THE CHAMPION IN YOU

Paul R. Hillman

Produced by:

FriesenPress

Suite 300 – 852 Fort Street
Victoria, BC, Canada V8W 1H8

www.friesenpress.com

Distributed to the trade by The Ingram Book Company

Table of Contents

Whatever you desire to become: you can;
if you believe that there is a champion in you.
Pursue it.

What does real life mean to a Champion? It is not the person you know in the fight—it is the person you don't know fighting you.

PREFACE:

To have real success in life, you will indeed go through some kind of hardship. Real life is defined by what you are willing to go through. This means that your character will be tested, your integrity will be challenged, and your faith proven. Whatever you are willing to achieve or choose to become in life, you must be willing to endure, whatever the situation that will come your way. The real test of your life comes to build you, to prove you, and to define the real person in you. Even the Lord Jesus Christ, who came as the way, the truth, and the life, had to go through a rugged cross, to give up His life, and to show the world what real life is about. Jesus came with a focus, and that was to do the will of His Father. It was not an easy road to Calvary, however, because He had a mind that was made up to accomplish His mission. The scripture tells us, "Looking unto Jesus, the author and finisher of our faith, who for the joy that was set before Him endureth the cross, despising the shame, and sat down at the right hand of the throne of God." (Hebrews 12:2) Jesus Christ came as the author of our faith, lived the life, endured the pain, and overcame the world before sitting down in His glory. He came and demonstrated what it means to achieve, what it means to become a Champion. If you are going to be victorious in becoming a Champion, you must be ready to endure pain, and go through your cross. Sometimes you will go through tears, bruises, sweat, and blood to define a Champion. The Bible gives a clear definition of faith in the book of Hebrews chapter 11. "Now faith is the substance of things hoped for, the evidence of things not seen." (Hebrews 11:1) Faith is to believe in yourself. In other words, you know that it is real, although it is not seen. Notice the scripture tells the readers that faith is a substance. Substance is a word which has mass, and occupies space. It is like baking a cake with all the good things on the inside, such as the ingredients. Although they are not seen after the cake is baked, all the ingredients together make the cake become perfect. Mass can be defined as something that rises. Imagine the yeast, or the baking powder, mixed with the ingredients in the cake; this helps the cake to rise. Although it is not seen, it makes a difference inside the cake. This is like activating your belief with your faith. Mass is also defines as a body, a group, a congregation, or a constitution. This means many minds coming together to make up the rules, or the law. In my own words, the substance of faith is powerful on the inside. Putting all the rules, mind, and laws together in one belief will become powerful, because there is power in agreement (Matthew 18:20, Acts 2:1). You can only overcome your fear by believing in your faith. The Bible declares that the heroes (or the Champions of faith), before they could become heroes and Champions, all went through things that were looking incredible and impossible. This means that for you to prove your faith, your work must be proven. The Bible tell us, "Faith without works is dead." (James 2:14-16) Your strength must be tested, your faith must be proven, and your flesh must go through some kind of affliction before bringing out the Champion that lives in you. Notice what the Bible says about Jesus after He went through the cross and His suffering: "And being found in the appearance as a man, He humbled Himself and became obedient to the point of death, even the death of a cross. Therefore God also has highly exalted Him and given Him the name which is above every name, that at the name of Jesus every knee should bow, of those in heaven, and of those on earth, and of those under the earth, and that every tongue should confess that Jesus Christ is Lord, to the glory of God the Father." (Philippians 2:8-10) Before Jesus Christ would be exalted to His glory, He went through something, emptied Himself before bringing out the power that was in Him. You will never know the power that is on the inside of you until you are ready to go the extra mile of emptying yourself. This is like going on a journey of faith. To test yourself by proving your faith, you have to surrender by giving up on your doubt. It is like the story of Abraham's journey when God told him to go and sacrifice his only son Isaac (Genesis 22). According to verse 4, Abraham, his son Isaac, and his servant went on a three-day journey. This means that Abraham had to go on a journey of faith, with his mind focused on his destiny, going through fatigue to reach his journey. After reaching his journey, he had to let go of himself, after binding his son and taking up his knife, as he was ready to kill Isaac (Genesis 22:10). After Abraham let go of everything in himself, the angel of God called out to Abraham, saying, "Lay not thine hand upon the lad, neither do thou anything unto him, for now I know that thou fearest God, seeing thou hast not withheld thy son, thine only son, from me." (Genesis 22:12) You will need to go through the fire of life to prove your value. Imagine a tea bag—there is value in a tea bag; it can be used as a medicine for some kind of symptom. However, if you don't put the tea bag through the hot water to boil the substance out, you will never get the use, the flavor, and the remedy from the inside to cure the symptom. Another illustration to look at is like baking a cake. You get all the ingredients such as spices like sugar, vanilla, raisins, fruits, baking powder, oil, eggs etc. You then mix them all together in flour, then put it all in a pan. However, unless you put the pan in the oven, you will never get a cake. To get the Champion out of you is like taking your strength, your heart, your mind, your character, your integrity, mixing them all with your faith, then going through the fire and the storms of life before bringing out the Champion that lives in you.

I chose to write this book because of my own life experience, and the many difficulties that I had to overcome as a fighter. The setbacks, the disappointment, the unfair management, and the many times that I had to fight for free, including giving up weight, and shedding a few pounds at the last minute before fight time. Those challenges, cuts, bruises, setbacks, and my many tears have helped me to understand that life is not defined by a walk in the park; life is not about a bed of roses. Real life is proven when you are willing to stand up and face your many adversities, the fear, the storms, and the many battles that will come up against you. Life is not about being lucky, or winning the lottery. Real life is defined by what you have been through, which proves the real you that lives on the inside. I did not only compete physically as a boxer—I have also been through some mental, emotional, and spiritual battles in my life. I started life on my own as an early teenager at the age of seventeen. I went through some early setbacks, had to make it over some cliffs and a bridge to escape death, and had to prove that God has a purpose for my life. At the age of fourteen, a bus turned over a cliff: I came very close to the point where I could have been killed—however, the Lord delivered me from dying in that bus over the cliff. At the age of seventeen, I went through a setback when the home that I was living in got burned down. I had to stay with a friend of mine until I could find a place of my own to stay. Some five years later, a hurricane struck the island, destroying the home that I was living in; it was a very hard time for people trying to survive in the rural area of Jamaica—however, God was watching over me. I could not become comfortable; I was force to make the best of life and become a survivor. During this time I did not know that there was a Champion on the inside of me. Life has thrown everything possible at me and I believed that it helped prepare me to become the person that I am today. I had to fight as a youth to survive in my school days. I remembered the days when I had to fight for my younger brothers during my young days in school. Little did I know the fights of my teenager days and the many fights and battles were just the beginning of a new era. The new era of my life is to be a fighter for the gospel of Jesus Christ: and to be the Champion of my destiny. I have learned through my life's journey and struggles that the things that come to knock me down and to keep me out of the things that God purposes for my life are the things that God has ordained for me to conquer, and for Him to use to bring the Champion out that lives in me. I take knowledge of the life of Jesus Christ that He lives on earth. He had to become a Champion for sinners, for those that are broken, and those that cannot save themselves. He had to die for the entire world. Not only would He have to die: He also had to rise from the dead to gain power, and to become the Champion of death. This means: He had to face His cross, carry His cross, and go through everything that the cross required, then die and rise again. Without going to the cross and dying, death could not be conquered. Without Jesus rising from the dead and becoming the resurrection of the dead, there could be no victory over death. He gave us the ability to go through the pain, the hurt: and everything that life brings to prepare you, so that you can rise up: and bring out the Champion that lives inside you. Life sometimes will take you to your limit and will force you to do something that also seems impossible; it is a time when you will become broken. This is when you must decide— either you are going to make it to your destiny, or give up on your destiny. It will be a time when your own mistakes takes you to that final moment of making a change that can better your life. You can take the example of the prodigal son in the gospel of Luke, chapter 15. Before he really came to himself, it was after he had gone through what I would call "the setback of his life"; he had now reached his point of brokenness, before realizing the mistake that he had made leaving home. A mistake in life will cause you to get in trouble, but sometimes your own mistakes help you to know better, giving you the option to make a change. This was when the prodigal son began speaking to himself. "And when he came to himself, he said, 'How many hired servants of my father have bread enough and to spare, and I perish with hunger?" (St. Luke 15:17) His mistake of leaving home had now taken him to a place of longing, a place of broken- ness, a place where he must either do, or die. This means that your mistakes in life give you a choice to either do better, or to stay in the same condition. Failing to correct your mistakes will let you become bitter, rather than getting better. According to the scriptures, God chastised those whom He loved (see Hebrews 12:6, Revelation 3:19, and Proverbs 3:12). This means that bringing out the Champion on the outside comes with discipline. You must be willing to take cor- rection, because it is a process of learning. There are many people that are living a life of too much comfort, and they fail to see the

Champion on the inside. To bring the Champion on the outside, your faith sometimes will be tested; you must be willing not to compromise, and you must be willing to push yourself to the next level. You see things different from the ordinary, because ordinary people will see the impossible, because the impossible makes it seems difficult. However, a Champion is one that sees the possibility, and is willing to do the extra-ordinary. When the Philistine Goliath came out to mock the Israelites, the army of Israel saw a giant, and were all terrified; however, David did not see a giant, and he did not see fear. What David saw was an uncircumcised Philistine (1 Samuel 17:26). Verse 24 of 1 Samuel 17 tells the readers that the men of Israel fled, and were sore afraid. A Champion does not look for an easy way out—he is one that does not make up words to deny himself from facing the battle. Bringing the Champion out of you will make a way to your destiny, but it comes with a step of faith. You must be ready to defy the negative, and see the positive. A Champion will suffer loss and setbacks, but that does not deny you from who you are within. Although I suffer many losses, they did not deny me from seeing my destiny, they rather helped me to see my way out, even when it looked impossible. It was sometime after the hurricane struck my home, where I suffered many losses; I went and joined a boxing gym in Negril, Jamaica. Nine months later I was a Champion for Jamaica. I went through an early setback after a motorbike that I was riding collided with a car. I was thrown from the motorbike approximately fifteen feet in the air, then fell over a bridge. I was unconscious for a moment, and also suffered a broken leg. I was later rushed to the emergency, but the Lord delivered me. It again happened five years later, on September 13, 1994. I was going to the Embassy when the bus rolled over three times, and again God came through for me when He delivered me from death. I went through many sad moments, many setbacks as a fighter, and unfair management to prove the real person in me. After I immigrated to Boston Massachusetts, I became Champion six consecutive times, and was two times the most outstanding boxer in the New England Boxing Championship, 1995-1996. After I turned professional, I went through many trainers and managers, because I found out that they did not care about me—they were just in it for the money. Although I went through a setback with my ex-wife, she was a very good woman to me. She was there for me in my many challenges, and always helped me to make the right decision. She has witnessed the many fights that were given on short notice, and the many times that I was asked to give up weight to the other fighter. I remember in my last fight in Boston: I was told two weeks before the fight that my opponent would be seven pounds heavy over the weight class that I was fighting. After giving up the seven pounds, two days before the fight, I was told that I would need to sell tickets to earn my salary. I told my manager that I would not fight for free, because I could not take two days selling tickets to make a salary. My wife then was worried that I would get in trouble if I refused to fight. She then told me to make it my last fight. Although I won in the second round with a TKO, I still did not get paid. I was out there trying to find a way for myself. I often wondered where my journey of faith would take me. I knew within myself that it was God who opened the door for me in getting to the United States of America—however, I did not know where my source of income would come from. I knew that boxing was my only option, and my determination was to be a Champion, and to prove to the world that I am someone to be recognized. I did not know that God had a plan and another purpose for me. Becoming a Champion to prove to the world would have me living in pride, and this was not what God desired for me. So I had to give up my boxing career before seeing the journey and the destiny that God had for me. Oftentimes, people decide to step out in life to do their own desire and forget God. However, if it is God's will for your life, you will have to give up the things that you desire, give up the things that look good, before God will give you the things that are best for you. You can take an example from the life of Abraham in Genesis 12. Before God would take Abraham to a place to bless him, Abraham had to first leave his comfort zone, and then he had to leave his family. Also, Abraham did not know where he was going, or the place that God was taking him. "Now the Lord had said to Abram, "Get thee out of thy country, and from thy kindred, and from thy father's house, unto a land that I will shew thee."

(Genesis 12:1) This means that before God will move you from your place of comfort, you must be willing to trust God for the outcome, even when you don't see the way of making your income. When God gets ready to bless your life, you must be ready to leave your place of comfort. Abram, whose name was later changed to Abraham, had to take a risk of faith to leave everything behind, and also to leave his father's house. This proves that God was his only Father and would become his Jehovah Jireh to provide the real source of income for Abraham's life. Before becoming the Champion that God desires you to be, you must be willing to give up your titles and belongings, and be willing to give up the name and the fame that you chose to claim. Whenever you give up everything of the world and follow God, God will make you become the Champion, and will give you a title that the world cannot give you. I remember when my wife back then would take me with her to Bible study every Wednesday evening: I decided to follow her advice and started going to Bible study with her, until I developed a passion for learning and studying God's word. I gave up my boxing career which I was hoping would help me in earning a living. I began putting my trust in God, trusting that He would open doors for me. After I gave up boxing, I joined a church called Union Baptist Church. I was very committed and dedicated in working for the Lord. Two years after joining that church, I was ordained as a deacon. After serving two years as a deacon, I was licensed to preach the Gospel of the Lord Jesus Christ. God had now taken me from a physical fight to a spiritual fight. I believed that my physical fight was only my preparation for dedication, and for the training of becoming a disciple for the Lord Jesus. Whenever God gets ready to bring the Champion out of you, God will take you through some setbacks, some tragedies, giving you something to test you, to move you, to prove you, and to prepare you for greatness, and to bring out the champion from the inside of you. Taken from a biblical view of the early life of David, we see that when he was only sixteen years old, the Lord sent the prophet Samuel to anoint him as the chosen king of Israel (1 Samuel 16:35): "Then Samuel took the horn of oil, and anointed him in the midst of his brethren, and the Spirit of the Lord came upon David from that day forward. So Samuel rose up, and went to Ramah." (11 Samuel 16:13). Before David was anointed by the prophet Samuel, he was a humble shepherd boy taking care of sheep. He had to go through his valleys, his lowest point before he could find himself at the place where God prepared for him to be. There are people who will never admire you, or see the greatness in you, when you are at your lowest point. However, God will put you at your lowest, or take you to a place of humility, because such a place becomes your place of preparation. Just like giving service, it is a place that you start before becoming great. It is the same way in becoming a Champion; sometimes before one becomes a Champion, it could start out with a knock-down, because your strength must be tested; your character must be proven, and you've got to be willing to handle the fear of your life in order to show the world what real life means, and what it is made of. What does real life mean to a champion?

Real life to a champion is like one who had to make his or her way out of a boxing ring, without seeing the way out. It is like fighting your way out of a cage fight. A boxing ring is not made with doors or windows, and it does not have a gate where you can walk out. The only way to get out of a boxing ring is to fight your way out. You get out of that ring by following the rules. You sometimes have to take a licking, and if you really want to be the champ, you've got to keep on jabbing, keep on moving, and scoring points. Your success will be tested, you will sometimes hit the canvas, and you will become bloody, but this is where you prove your strength and character. It is not the many knock-downs that you receive as a fighter that matters; what really matters is the amount of times that you choose to get up and fight back. Your sweetest victory comes when the battle becomes intensified, a time when you were about to be counted out, but were able to turn the fight around into your favor. This means your knock-down only comes to test the Champion in you. You might have been through some mental knock-downs, or some emotional knock-downs. You might have suffered some hurt, some pain and some setbacks trying to go forward—however, God brought you out of them and used the same setback and knock-downs to strengthen you so that you can go forward. It is up to you to use all the things you have been through as your tools to bring out the Champion. Let the world see the real you. Sometimes people will call you a loser because of your failures or your mistakes. You don't need to let people tell you about who you are; you are the one that decides your destiny, you decide what you will become. This means that failures and mistakes are not your option, they are just your learning guide. Not because you find yourself on the rope, or have been on the defense; that does not disqualify the Champion in you. Being on the rope gives you a better view of the fight—it helps you to see your opponent's mistakes, and also helps you to counter your opponent. This then means that being on the rope can be your best offense. You can use it as a way of countering the counter. Your best defense is your strongest offense. Whatever you are willing to go through will decide what you are willing to become; your strength must be tested, and you must be ready to face the giant of your life—not because you lost some fights, not because you have been down, been hurt, or been given up on. God will use those things to show His glory in your life. God will use your setbacks to prove your comeback, and that they were just your testimonies to impact the lives of those who have gone through the same tragedies in life. Remember, the word of God tells us, "The stone which the builder refused has become the headstone of the corner. This is the Lord's doing; it is marvelous in our eyes." (Psalm 18:22-23, KJV). God is looking for a Champion who is willing to please God, one who represents the character of God, and does not put his or her confidence in man's power, or the world, but in the confidence of God. This was the reason for David to say, "The Lord is on my side; I will not fear—what can man do unto me?" (Psalm 118:6)I in addition, "It is better to trust in the Lord than to put confidence in princes." (Psalm 118:9) A Champion does not run from the battle—he is one that run towards the battle. He is one that make sure that the job gets done by following the rules and regulations. A Champion is one who works very hard to achieve the best. This means you don't accept failures, you rather accept challenges. Notice in the life of David that he did not run from the challenge of Goliath; he went forward to face the giant. He did not look as one that fits the battle, because a Champion must not be judged by his or her looks, which I will mention in another chapter. You are not the real you when you are acting or pretending. You are not what people see when they look at you from the outward appearance. The real you is when you are not aware of what you are doing. It is like sleeping—you do not know what you are doing when you are sleeping. The Champion in you sometimes sleeps; if you are pushed to the limit, whatever is on the inside of you will be ready to come out. I remember as a young boxer doing push-ups with my boxing trainer; there was not a set number of push-ups—I would have to keep going until I had nothing left. Whenever you stretch yourself, or push yourself to your limit, you are only making room for yourself to go further. A Champion does not go backward, he is one that is ready to go forward; he resists fear, and steps out by faith. He is always ready to face the crowd with a pleasing performance, by bringing out his best. He does not become dismayed, or moved by boos and jeers of the crowd, he rather stays humble, and keeps his or her focus. I remembered fighting out of my hometown where I was booed a few times. I was booed because I was not considered the crowd favorite, because I was fighting the crowd's hometown hero. However, I did not let their booing and jeering distract me—all I did was keep my focus, believing in the person in me. After the fight, I became the star and the hometown hero. A Champion is one who does not goes to sleep in school, because he or she knows that school teaches the golden rules, and the tools: That person will graduate with all the requirements that are needed, such as endurance, discipline, dedication, perseverance, and faith to prove yourself. In addition, he or she will stand up for what is right and speak the things that are true. Your potential as a Champion is to master every area that you faces with. As I oftentimes say, "A master student does not run from his challenge, he is one that embraces his challenge." Wherever a Champion is weak, that will be the area he or she will be more challenged with the obstacles of life. The enemy's plan is for you to defeat the Champion in you, however, God's desire is to use the Champion in you to defeat the giants that always present themselves before you, such as the things that bring fear. This means that no one else can beat the Champion in you, but you. No one can tell you that you can't; no one can stop you, but yourself. The only time they can stop you is if you believe them, which means you have to believe in your-self. I think back over my journey of faith, the rural area that I came from, and the ways in which I grew up in Jamaica, the opposition that I encountered, the many battles that I fought in my physical fights, and the many times when I was told that I would get beaten; however, I did not let those words deny the Champion in me, because I choose to believe in myself. I think back in this passage when my father told me that I could not make it in Boston Massachusetts, after leaving Jamaica on my own: I did not have any family in Boston, and did not have any money in my pocket, which makes it becomes a risky move. Although I did not have the financial tools, I did already knew that I had the physical tools, along with the Character that I did need to make it. I leave on the word which my grandmother, the late Annie Bowen, told me: She said to me one day, "Son, whenever you step out in life, always step out on faith, and put God first, and He will direct your way." These were the same words that I told my father, saying, "Papa, I am stepping out in faith. God will open doors for me." As long as you take a step of faith, God will direct your feet to take two. Sometimes you will fall or go through setbacks, but God will never leave you to stay down. He will pick you up with His strong right hand (Psalm 37:23-24). It was the dis-ciple whose name was Simon Peter that stepped out of the boat into the storm to walk towards Jesus (Matthew 14:22-30). Although he had doubted and was about to go down, Jesus stretched out His hand of mercy and saved Peter. The endurance, the dedication, and the discipline that is in me, those characteristics are things that helps me to be the person that I am today, which also helps me to write this book to let the readers know, "There is a Champion in you." Yes, you will get some kind of knock-down in life, and surely you will have some kind of setback, but these are the things that will defines the Champion in you, and will give you the definition of a Champion. They did not happen to deny you, but rather, they came to build you, and to prepare you for the Champion that God created you to be. Remember what the Bible tells us about perseverance—you must count at all joy when your faith has been tested (James 1:2-3). Count it all joy when you have been pressed, even to the point of feeling depressed. It is through these trials of life that God prepares and equips you for a greater purpose. God oftentimes takes us through the physical pains and emotions before bringing us to our spiritual rest. Your physical knock-downs in life are happening because they give you the strength that will prepare you for the next level of your destiny. God is getting you ready to show you things that you have never seen before, to take you place that you have never gone before, and to give you a crown that you have never received before. This book is to let you know, you have to endure affliction, and you have to master your challenge. If your mind is made up, you will be the best that you can be; you will be able to defeat your own fear, defeat the fear of life, and prove who God made you to be—and that will bring out the Champion in you.

This book is to get you stirred up; you will never know about the power that lies within you until you start climbing, start digging, and start exhaling to the next level that seems impossible. Whenever someone tell you that you can't, that's just a test for you to prove God by telling yourself, "I can do all things through Christ Jesus, who strengthened me." (Philippians 4:13) I pray that after you finish reading this book, you will see yourself more determined in making a step of faith, taking on the impossible, and bringing out the Champion that God created on the inside of you.

It is not the person you know in the fight—it is the person you don't know fighting you:

Whenever one encounters a fight, he or she may look at the fight from a natural appearance—or a physical appearance—assessing the looks, the build, the muscles, or the physique, without knowing the person's plans, his tricks, his intentions, or his abilities. No one goes to battle without a plan or some secret weapon. There's got to be something that your enemy or your opponent does not know about. In a fight, don't you ever take it simple (which I will also discuss in a later chapter called "Don't watch the look—read the book.") It is not about what your thoughts are, or what you know you can do—you also need to know about the person standing in front of you, and what he or she is capable of. It is like the South Eastern Conference football league; any college team can be beaten on any given day. When you look at a giant, he may seem to be a giant on the outside, yet there is a chicken on the inside; this is the same way you should look at someone that looks on the outside. He or she may look like a chicken on the outside, but there could be a giant on the inside. It is not the person that you see standing in front of you, it is the person that stand inside the person you see in front of you. This is to let you know that the secret to your success is an inside preparation. You may not know the person that you are fighting, but if you know the person fighting you, then you will take a different approach to the fight, rather than just looking at the person that comes to fight you. There is a phrase that says, "It is not the dog in the fight, it is the fight in the dog." It is not the person that you are competing with that you should prepare for—you should prepare for the person you don't know that lives on the inside. A Champion does not show him or herself until when they had to dig deep. You can never be a Champion if you don't go above or beneath, or go the extra mile. You have to be ready in your mind to face the fear, and to know that the real fight is not just the physical fight—the real fight is a spiritual fight that comes from within. The Bible tells us, "For we wrestle not against flesh and blood, but against powers, against the rulers of the darkness of this world, against spiritual wickedness in high places." (Ephesian 6:12) This verse lets us know that the real fight takes place in the dark; it takes place in the mind, and in places beyond our own imagination or understanding. Don't just look at the person that you see in the natural—the Bible is telling us about a spiritual fight. Whenever you approach a spiritual fight, you should know that there will be some tricks, some tactics, and some deception; this means you have to gear up yourself in the word of God, and put on the whole armor (verse 13-17). In every fight, spiritual or physical, there's got to be a preparation to face the unexpected, because the enemy or opponent will be coming with a plan to counter, a plan to attack, a plan to hurt you, a plan to deceive you, and a plan to destroy you. This goes back to my first book, "The Spiritual Battle With the Mind". Your enemy or opponents will be coming with an unthinkable strategic plan, and that is to counter the plan in your mind. If your enemy or opponent knows what you are thinking, he will try to counter your plan. The best way to beat a counter puncher is to counter the counter puncher. In other words, you sometimes have to play a fool to be wise. It is more important to know the person fighting you than to just know the person that you are fighting. The enemy that comes to fight you is not the one you see on a daily basis. The Judas that sits at your table, eating and drinking with you, is not the one you thought was your friend; the real Judas is the one that is planning to betray you on the inside. A former friend of mine, who was also a fighter, knew me as a friend, but he did not know about the fighter in me, until one day he decided to fight me. He thought that he was the better fighter, until after he was TKO in the third round. It is not about who you know on the outside, it is about who you know living on the inside, then you will know that Champions are those that live from within.

THE REAL FIGHT FROM WITHIN:

There are people who look at fights from the physical; the natural fight that happens in their daily live. The fights that happen in the street; the fights that happen at home; the fights of boxers that compete in the boxing ring. However, the real fight of life is the fight that takes place from within. The storms of life, the fatigue of your journey, the bills that come at you on a monthly basis—these things can be considered as emotional injuries, and physical injuries from the real fight on the outside. The physical fights of life are not your real fight—they are just the build-up for the real test, and the real fight on the inside. The real fight begins after you are fatigued on the inside, after you are overwhelmed, when you are bleeding on the inside of your heart; it comes through the fears in your mind, and the many tears that flow from your eyes. You may have seen people that triumph, and dominate the physical fight that they encountered, just because they are physically strong. You could be winning the physical fight of your life, or the things that confront you in your daily struggle; this is where the Devil will also try to trick you. His desire is for people to see you winning the natural fight; they may have watched your hands raised high in the air—however, they don't see the fear in your mind, and they don't see you bleeding in the heart as it continues to beat. They may see you smile on the outside, but have never seen you crying behind closed doors. His desire is to fight you from within, because within is the place where he wants to keep you in isolation, where you don't know what to do; his plan for you is to give up the fight that you are dealing with from within. I can remember some years ago while working at a La fitness club as a trainer, I saw a young man working out on one treadmill. This young man was looking to be in great shape; he was all muscular, looking really fit and healthy as if he did not need to be working out in the gym. I watched him as he was working out, doing his cardio, but I could tell that he was dealing with something in himself. It seemed as if he was fighting a battle in his mind, something that he seemed to be wrestling with. I then went up towards him and begin a conversation, just to talk about real life's issues, and sure enough, there were some real life issues that this young man was dealing with that I would call "The real fight from within." Of course this young man did not need a physical trainer, or a personal trainer, but he did really need a spiritual and emotional trainer. He began telling me about the fight that he was dealing with from within, as he opened up in tears. His wife had divorced him, leaving him with the bills and other affairs that he was struggling with. His new girlfriend that he was dating became ill and suddenly had died. This young man showed up in the gym as if he needed a workout, but he did not need a workout—he needed a word from God within, because the Devil was giving him a fight from within. A real Champion does not fight from the outside, he is one that fights from within, because his strength lies on the inside. If you are going to become an overcomer, you must first learn to overcome the external affairs of life, because those things that happen on the outward come to strengthen the inwardly. It was the Apostle Paul who said in one of his letters, "Though the outward man perishes, the inward man renews daily." (2 Corinthians 4:16). Whenever you can win the fights from within by using your faith, and the things concerning the word of God, this is when you will be able to prove that there is a Champion in you. You will have to fight with your mind, fight with your heart, fight with your strength, and use all the tools on the inside that build up your faith. Whenever you can master the fight from within, your fight on the outside will become your pushover. Before facing your challenge on the outside, you must first challenge yourself on the inside. This means to sharpen all your God-given tools. God knows that the Devil can only fight you from the outside, by using thing to get to the inside, and this is why He prepares you on the inside. If your tools on the inside are not sharpened and prepared to face your outside fight, then you are in trouble facing the Devil when he begins throwing things at you. Your inside preparation comes through praying, fasting, studying, reading the word of God, and by building a closer relationship with God. The same ways in which you train for your physical fight are the same ways in which you are required to train for your spiritual fight. Just as you train on the outside to build muscles, so must you train on the inside to build faith muscles, because faith without works is dead (see James 2:26). A battle that is considered spiritual is not fought on the outside—it is fought on the inside. This means that the preparation for the real battle of life begins within you. You may wonder why you had to spend time going through your physical preparation—just like going through four years of college, all the things that you go through on the outside is what prepares you on the inside. The hours that you stayed in the gym, the hours that you stayed in class to prepare yourself were because you were building character, you were building some form of definition on the inside. It is the same in spending time in the Word of God, communicating with God on a daily basis, spending time in prayer, and building a closer relationship with God. People may have look at you, judge you from the outward appearance, and some might have thought about the things that you have to face in life. They don't know where you find the strength and the courage to deal with them, but they don't see the strength and the things that you developed on the inside. Someone could look strong on the outside, or look muscular, because that person was born looking physically strong, or just because of his genetic shape—however, without going through the preparation on the inside, that person will have difficulty handling the fight on the outside. Think about the many times that you had to cry, the times that you suffered hurt, setbacks, and heartbreak, these are things that happen in your life to prepare you for your real fight when the Devil comes at you.

Remember, when the Devil afflicted Job, he stripped Job of the things that he possessed on the outside. He was trying to change Job from the person that he was on the inside. He thought that he could change Job's faith, and the person he was in God, but did not know about the faith and the strength that lies on the inside towards God. He afflicted Job by stripping him of everything, even the flesh that was on his body (Job 2:7-8). It did seem as if Job had nothing on the outside to fight with, nothing to live for, because he was too weak, and everything was gone from him. The real fight of Job's life now seemed as if it had started on the inside. This was where he had to struggle to maintain his faith and integrity. This was the reason why his wife asked him, "Dost thou still retain thine integrity? Curse God, and die" (Job 2:9). However, Job held on to his faith and fought in the inner man. "Though the outward man perishes, the inward man renews daily" (2nd. Corinthians 4:16). Your real fight never starts until your faith is challenged, when everything seems to be falling apart. You have to bring out the best from the inside. This is when your real fight begins, when you have to prove your inner strength. Things will come to test your faith on the outward, but it is not the way they seem one the outside that matters—what really matters is the way in which you look at them from the inside. Jesus Christ was tempted by the Devil when He was asked by the Devil to turn stones into bread (St. Matthew 4:3). Although Jesus had the power to turn stones into bread, He did not need to show His power on the outside to please the Devil; His focus was about what lives on the inside, and that was to do the work of His Father, and to please God in His word. This was why He told the Devil, "It is written, 'Man shall not live by bread alone, but by every word that proceedeth out of the mouth of God.'" (St. Matthew 4:4 KJV—also, see Deuteronomy 8:3.) The temptation, the test, and the trials of life are things that God uses to prepare the inner-man. Although God does not tempt anyone, He uses the trials that the Devil uses to afflict us with, those that cause conflict in our lives, to give us spiritual strength. You would not have known your inner strength, and the Champion living on the inside, if you have never been tested on the outside. You would not have known the power on the inside of you if you always depended on someone to help you up, rather than you trying to help yourself! It is after you have been left on your own, after you have been put into some kind of hole, or pit, left there alone to fight your way out. This is when you realized that you had to use every muscle, and all the strength on the inside, with your determination, and faith muscles to pull yourself out. It has been told in a story that I heard about a certain donkey. This donkey was too old to live; the owner tried to get rid of the donkey by putting the animal into a hole, with the intention to bury the donkey alive. It happened that while the owner tried to cover the donkey in the hole with dirt, the donkey shook the dirt off its back, then used the same dirt to build a solid ground on which to rise out of the hole. The things that the enemy tries to use to bury you, God will use the same things to strengthen you, so that you can rise out of that situation. Remember what the Bible said about the children of Israel who were in bondage in Egypt under the leadership of Pharaoh: "But the more they afflicted them, the more they multiplied and grew. And they were grieved because of the children of Israel." (Exodus 1:12 KJV) The reason that the Egyptians were grieved was because despite all they did to afflict the children of Israel: it seemed as if they were helping them. Despite the circumstances that you will go through in life, you can rise out of those things, and use them as a preparation to your destiny. Trials and afflictions can be seen as your preparation. It was the Psalmist David who said, "Before I was afflicted I went astray, but now I have kept thy word." (Psalm 119:67KJV) Here it seems as if David uses his affliction as a lesson. Although he did not know, and did not understand why he had to go through it, it left him with a divine conjunction: "But now I have kept thy word." Affliction and chastisement are a learning process to your destiny; in addition, they are the tools that will equip you in bringing out the Champion in you. It was after the process of his affliction that he went on further to say these words: "It is good for me that I have been afflicted, that I might learn that statutes." (Verse 71) Every affliction that you have gone through, they are just your learning process. The many times that you cried, the times that you tripped over something, all the past hurt, the tears and fears, they are just you process your development in preparing the

Champion that lives in you. I did not know that there was a book on the inside of me, much less two. I did not know that I could pay the bills all by myself until I was left alone to struggle. It was after I had to fight from within, with no one to help me, with no one to fight for me—that's when I found out that a Champion was living inside of me. I remember the night after I was on my own: Two friends of mine took me out to a restaurant to eat. I did not have any money in the bank; all I had in my pocket was eight dollars. After going to the restaurant, I was expecting my friends to pay my bill, but they both went up to the counter and paid for their meals, leaving me standing alone. I then had to go to the counter, look at the menu and order a meal that was cheaper than eight dollars, including tax. After all three of us sat down eating, the Lord spoke to my spirit, saying, "I want to show you who is with you when you have no one on your side." God had to remind me that He is the only one that I had to stand with me, when everyone departs and leaves me alone. For you to know that God is the only one that will be with you when you are in trouble, it will be a time when you are going through your valley. You will indeed go through your valley before you can write your story. I think to myself about David, his life and testimonies, and the many Psalms that he wrote in the Bible. I often think to myself, where did David get these words to write all these Psalms? I have now learned that David got these Psalms in his time of valleys—he used his valleys as a place of reflection. Although he was a shepherd in his valley watching the sheep, he began to reflect on himself as the sheep, while God, the good shepherd, was watching him, keeping him, and also protecting him in his valleys. This was the reason =he said, "The Lord is my shepherd; I shall not want." (Psalm 23:1) David began to reflect that God placed him in the valley to bless him; God used his valley as a place of preparation, a place of restoration, a place for his anointing, and a place to feed him in the midst of his enemies. It was through his valley that God prepared him to become the Champion that he was, and when he would leave his valley, he would never be alone, but was followed by goodness and mercy all the days of his life, and would dwell in the house of the Lord forever. Joseph, whom I also described as a Champion for God, went through his own valley. He could not become the prince of Egypt before he was prepared in his valley. It was after he had made it out of his pit and his prison, described in Genesis 37: 24 and chapter 39 verse 20. It was through his pit and his prison he developed his wisdom, his knowledge and understanding before becoming a leader, and a prince in the land of Egypt. God allowed him to go through a place that prepared him, a place of affliction before he could receive the promotion, and the revelation that God revealed unto him for his destiny, described in Genesis 37:7-10. Whatever situations you encounter in your life's journey, don't let those things deny the Champion that lives in you—see those things as your preparation in bringing out the Champion that lives in you. You were already born to be the Champion that God created you to be, but sometimes it takes many setbacks, and many comebacks, to prove what you were made of, so that people can see you as the extra-ordinary. The Champion that lives in you is like a seed that is planted for destiny, a seed that surrounded with weeds and other things that will come to try oppose the seed from sprouting, and from growing to be that tree. Just as cutting the weeds, plowing the lawn, and doing the things that are necessary to bring that seed to a tree that brings forth fruit, it is the same with the Champion in you. You will need to use your gifts, your skills, your desire, your determination, your strength, and your faith to oppose everything that comes to stop you from bring-ing out the Champion from within.

THE REAL FIGHT OF A CHAMPION:

The real fight of a Champion is when you really believe in who you are on the inside. You cannot fight like a Champion if you don't believe that you are a Champion. This means that you would enter the fight with doubt on the inside that you are who you are on the inside. This is why fear comes from the outside. Whenever two fighters come face-to-face, they are looking for the fear on the outside by looking in each other's eyes. You could look simple on the outside, but what really matters is who you are on the inside, and the person that lives in you. The Bible tells us, "Greater is He that is in you than he who is in the world" (1 John 4:4). The enemy of this world does not want you to know that there is a Champion living in you. His desire is to see you walking in fear; easily shaken by words. His plan for you is to live a life of feeling defeated and depressed. A Champion does not live by the way he or she feels, because feeling is a vowel. If a Champion judges someone by the way the person looks; and the way he or she feels, then he or she would be setting themselves up to fail. For you to bring out the Champion that lives in you, you have to first believe in yourself; believe in the God that lives in you; and believe that you were born as an overcomer. The Bible already tells us that believers, "…were born of God, and have overcome them" This scripture is talking about overcoming the evil one known as the devil. If you are a believer in God, you were born to overcome the obstacles that will oppose you in your life's journey. (1 John 4:4). You were already a Champion before you were born; you did not make yourself a Champion, the Champion was already in you. All the great athletes that became Champions did not see the gifts, and the Champion they were, because gifts and Champions are not seen from the outside: they all come from the inside. How did they become Champions on the outside? How did they prove their gifts and talents on the outside? They first had to take a step of faith by facing their challenge by stepping out of themselves, stepping out of their fear, then facing their challenges, their giants, and the obstacles that were standing in their way. Without stepping out, they would not know the person living on the inside. If you choose to live in fear, you will accept whatever the enemy says about you. Fear will tell you that you are a loser. If you fail to believe in the Champion within, you will believe the enemy. The real gift in you is not the package on the outside. The package can be looking good on the outside, well-tailored and looking valuable, but the value of the package is about the gift that is on the inside. You can open a package that looks very prestigious and well-tailored, but after opening the package, you then found out that it is just an empty package. In addition, you can open a package that was not wrapped in a prestigious way, nor looked gorgeous on the outside, only to find the best gift and most wonderful treasure on the inside. There are people who fail to open the package; some refuse the package, because it is not well-tailored, nor does it look like a gift, or perhaps it did not come in a large parcel. This is why you should not judge from the outside. You should not judge a person by look—it's like reading a book before making judgment. You don't think or feel that there is a Champion in you—you have to believe in yourself. Sometimes people will try to put doubt in you; this is when you speak to yourself, when you are feeling discouraged. Whenever you are in doubt, believe in yourself by speaking the following words: "There is a Champion living inside of me!" "Greater is He that is in me, than he that is in the world," "I can do all things through Christ Jesus, which strengthened me," "I am more than a conquerer through Him that loves me." Remember that life and death is in the power of your tongue

(Proverbs 18:21). This means that whatever you speak and believe is very powerful (see St. Mark 11:23-24). Believe by faith, then move by faith. Start climbing your mountain by exercising your faith; get ready to face your giant. Wherever you face your biggest challenge that is the place your Champion lives. If you overcome an obstacle that seemed to be a pushover, it is because you did not give it your best. If you did not beat the best; don't expect to be the best. If you did not exercise your faith, it means you did not challenge your fear. To challenge your fear, you have to be willing to embrace your challenge. Don't look for an easy fight; don't look for an easy win. Always look for ways to improve; this means that you have to be willing to prove yourself so that you can improve. The only way to bring the Champion out is to beat the giant, or the so-called champion in front of you. Even if you have to get knocked down a few times, get back up to fight again. You will not know how much you have in you to prove until after you find yourself getting up from off the canvas. You would not try so hard in life unless you had experienced defeat and setbacks. People will never appreciate the things that are very important in their lives, until those things are all taken away. You must come to the point of understanding that no one will give you the things that you need to make it in life, unless you bring everything that you have on the inside out. This is the same mentality you need to have going into the fight of your life. The real fight of a true Champion is when he is on his way back to the top, after losing it all before. A person who perhaps had a setback in prison, where he meditated every day, or spent time to gather his or her focus. Read books about coming back, do all different kinds of pushups and sit-ups. This will be a person who will be coming back with vengeance, with one aim, and one determination. He or she will enter the ring with all the necessities, all the instruments, all the tools, and all the learning guides that setbacks teach. Every challenge that you encountered, you can use them to define the real you on the inside. Can you imagine losing everything that you need to survive, going to the bottomless pit, and then getting a chance to regain what you lost? The return of a Champion after losing it all is like a drowning person lunging to a straw to save his or her own life. He or she learns the value of being down, and the strength that it takes to get back on their feet, and knows that failures are a learning process. They are your defeat, they are just your keys to success. In addition, they are also your corrections to your mistakes. You will be able to return with all the words, the proverbs, and the wisdom that life teaches. "The hotter the battle, the sweeter the victory," "The race is not for the swift, nor the battle for the strong, but for the one that endures to the end," "If I can take it, then I can make it," "The height by great men reach and kept were not attained by sudden flight, but they, while their companions slept, they were toiling upward through the night." Joseph in the Bible had a setback after he was framed by his master's wife, and was cast into a dungeon. He did not go to high school or college. He first went to a pit when his own brothers left him there to suffer, then was removed from the pit and sold into slavery. He then found favor before had a setback and was thrown into a dungeon. He got his education from what I call the high school of pit, to the college of dungeon. It was in the dungeon, a place of setback, where God took him and prepared him with all the tools and wisdom. After graduating from the dungeon, he had the tools and wisdom to interpret dreams. He told Pharaoh the meaning of seven fat cows versus seven thin cows. From his place of setback and preparation, he later became a ruler, and a prince over the land of Egypt. The same brothers that sold him into Egypt were the same brothers who came back and bowed down to him. In other words, he became their Champion. A Champion discovers the greatness that he or she has on the inside through defeat, pain, setbacks, and the places of brokenness. You will never know the Champion that lives on the inside if you have never defeated the setbacks, the opposition, and the giants that come to stop you. You cannot beat the giant by going around in circles looking for a way out. Your only option is to take the giant down—take away his or her crown, and prove to the world that a Champion is one that stands alone. A true Champion is one who get knocked down, but refuses to stay down. He or she will get up, fight back, and then prove to the world that a true Champion is unstoppable. This also goes for emotional and mental setbacks. There are people who went through setbacks in relationships and are not allowed to live with their children. This happens to some fathers, after going through the setbacks of divorce. Some give up on their children: some refuse to pay child support. A real man who proves himself to be the Champion of setbacks is one who refuses to give up on his children—one who will work two and three jobs to support his children. This will prove the real father, the real man, and the real Champion that God created him to be. It will seem as if setbacks come to deprive you of the things that God gave you. However, setbacks can also be used as a tool to bring out the real person in you. If you have never suffered failures, heartbreak and pain, you would never know what it means to be healed and to be restored again. In addition, you would not know the meaning of fighting back, and learning from your own failures and mistakes. David suffered a setback, and was heartbroken when he got Bathsheba—the wife of Uriah—pregnant; he then set up Uriah to die. It was after this setback—and this place of brokenness—that he returned with a desire and a passion to know God. He had come to a place of humility, and a place of knowing the knowledge of God. Setbacks and heartbreak will put you at the mercy seat of God. In Psalms 51, David cried out to God for mercy, because his setbacks helped him to understand that he was not perfect. In addition, it also helped him to understand the mercy of God. It forced him to make a comeback, to clean up his mess. He prayed a sincere prayer that truly comes from the depth of his heart: "Have mercy upon me, O God, according to thy loving kindness; according to thy tender mercies, blot out my transgressions. Wash me thoroughly from mine iniquity, and cleanse me from my sin. For I acknowledge my transgression, and my sin is ever before thee." (Psalm 51:3) His mess led him to brokenness; his brokenness then led him to repentance, and his repentance led him to restoration. One of the first steps in the process of restoration in the life of a Champion is to acknowledge the area that he or she went wrong. In David's return, he acknowledged his transgressions; he could never hide his sin from God. (Psalm 51:3) Mistakes and setbacks will point out your weakness, but it is up to you to identify and to correct them. In becoming the Champion that God created you to be, you must confess your weakness before God, and acknowledge your mistakes. David's own mess took him to a place of knowing wisdom, and gave him a heart that God seeks from those who fear Him, according to Psalm 51:17. He understand from his own mess that God seeks truth from the inward, as said in verse 6. Before his sin was revealed by the prophet Nathan, he was keeping it as a secret, which would have caused him to become blind in knowing the wisdom, and the things concerning God. In addition, it was through his setback that he could now teach sinners the way of the Lord. This was the reason he said in verse 13, "Then will I teach transgressors thy ways, and sinners shall be converted unto thee." (Psalms 51:13) It was after his spiritual, emotional, and physical failures that he came to himself, just like the prodigal son in St. Luke chapter 15:11; he learned a lesson: Restoration comes through the process of being broken. David's heart was now contrite before God, and he was ready to come, open and broken before GodI. In other words, this time, David was for real. God seeks a heart that is contrite before Him, and a spirit that is broken. According to the scripture, He will not turn away the broken spirit and the heart that is contrite, as written in Psalms 51:17. Whenever you are broken before God, you will do whatever is necessary and whatever is pleasing to God. Before the breaking point, some folks will mess around; some will become comfortable doing things that are pleasing in their own eyes, because they are not real before God. However, coming back to God from being broken (or from a setback) forces you to become more serious. You also become vulnerable, and are ready to open up every secret area of your life before God. This is why God seeks after a heart that is contrite. You must be real before God if you are going to get the solution that you desperately need. A real Champion is one that refuse to hold back. He is one that is ready to let go, and go all out to give his or her best. You have to give your best before God, if you are going to receive the best. The Bible tells us to "Present our body as a living sacrifice, holy and acceptable unto God, for this is our reasonable service" (Romans 12:1). Giving your best with all your soul, might and strength and having nothing left proves you to be a true Champion. A true Champion can be defines in many ways, however there is a better example to defines a true

Champion. A true Champion is one who beats the champ. You can look at it from a boxing point view: You have the WBA (World Boxing Association), you have the WBC (World Boxing Council), and you have the IBF (the International Boxing Federation). There is a champion for each category—however to define the real champion as the undisputed champion, all three must fight before declaring the true champion, which means there is one true Champion. To be the true Champion that God created you to be is to beat the champ, and to become the undisputed Champion. A true Champion is one that will go through the storm, the fire, and the smoke of life—and when the calm and the smoke is clear, he or she will left standing alone. He or she is one who will not run away from the battle. Jesus Christ came and defines the meaning of a true Champion, by mastering His challenge, and receiving the crown of life. Although His disciples fled and left Him, He walked boldly to face His challenge and declared Himself to be who He really was (see St. John 18:4–8). This also means that a true Champion knows his or her purpose, and is one who serves this purpose. So many so-called champions bear the name, but are not willing to play the game. To play the game means you are willing to stand in the face of adversities, willing to face the storms that bring the fear of life, and are willing to make a change in the storm. In addition, he is one that does not look for an easy way out, but is one who is willing to stand in the gap, bind the gap, and to prove themselves. Some so-called champions are those who choose their opponents, and because of their opponent's resume, or record, they look for an easy win, or an easy payday. A true Champion takes on the best, and is willing to prove himself, and to make the necessary corrections to his weakness. While teaching Sunday school, I was making references to Genesis 3:2, while telling the class about God telling Adam and Eve not to touch or eat from the tree that was in the midst of the Garden of Eden. It was in the middle of Sunday school when my wife said, "Did God said they were not to touch it?" It seemed as if she was trying to oppose, or to interject; however, I then said to the class, "Let's go to the scripture." A student went to the scripture, read it and said, "He is right!" I did not take my wife's interjection as any form of opposition—rather, I took it as a way of keeping me on my guard, or on my toes. A true Champion must be ready to face the unexpected, and be ready to submit to the challenge of life with humility.

The race of a Champion:

A race can start out on a fast pace, or it can start out on a slow pace—the view of the outcome of a race is about getting to the finish line. Some people enter a race to win, while some are just in the race for a finish. There are other ways to define a race—it could be getting to the final point, or getting to the end of something. It can be a race of speed, or a race that you choose to run slowly. However, as I stated, it is about getting to the end of your race. What is the race of a Champion? The race of a Champion is a race that they are well-prepared to run. A Champion does not define his or her race by speed. He does not define his or her race by looking at the competitors, or the distance, but rather defines the race by his preparation. He or she spends time to gather all the tools, and the necessary needs that are vital for the race. So many started a race at a blazing speed, which can be good, but it depends on the distance. So many are excited to get to the finish line. Many look at the prize, but forget what it takes to get to the prize. Getting to the prize does not always come by speed—it comes with hard work, discipline and dedication. In other words, you have to work on your speed. Some athletes born with speed, however there are athletes who works on their speed, although they were born with speed; this makes them becomes even faster. The race of a Champion is not a short race, it is not a race of speed alone, his race comes with toiling, discipline, dedication, and working even harder to become much faster. Before getting to the finish line, you must first think about the cost: before building a home, you must first have a plan, the resources that are needed, and the time it will take to get done, which means you will also needed sufficient and skillful workers. Having the workers without the right tools could become a waste of time. Having the tools without the workers means that nothing will ever get done. Preparation also comes with a balance. You could be fast, but still you cannot last. The race of a Champion is a race that is well-balanced, and it is like calculating time and distance. He has to prepare for the distance by using the time that is required. Many people waste time by staying at a place where they become too comfortable. The place of a Champion is a place of preparation, a place to dream for the outcome. He or she understand that time plus place will add up to their place of destiny. His place for the race is a place of getting ready, rather than taking life easy. He does not have time to get lazy—his time is to prepare, then rest when the battle is finally over. Whenever a Champion shows up for a race, he or she shows up as the star, because he knows that he has all the requirements, such as the tools, the wisdom, and the courage. He is not just in as a competitor—a Champion is always in for a win, because he shows up with all the things that are required to win from within. Many start out in the race, but fade by the way. They entered the race without going through the process of preparation. It is a very sad feeling to know that you showed up unprepared—in other words, you showed up dis-qualified. A person who shows up disqualified is like one who shows up in fear, without having the faith to go all the way. It reminded me about the ten virgins that went out to meet the Bridegroom, in St. Matthew 25:1-13. The five virgins that were foolish did not bring any oil in their lamps (verse 3). In my own words, they did not go through the preparation to receive the stamina that was needed for the race that they were competing in. Perhaps they thought that the race was like a hundred, or a two-hundred-meter sprint. Even if it was, they would still mess up for not bringing any stamina, because the other five did; even if the five virgins were born to be sprinters as the foolish, they would have chosen to go through the preparation which would have made them become even more faster. Because the foolish virgins did not prepare themselves to gain stamina, they were not prepared to go all the way. Although both wise and foolish virgins went to sleep because the Bridegroom tarried, the five wise virgins did have energy, or stamina, that was reserved, because they went through the preparation—however, the foolish virgins did not have any. When the Bridegroom showed up, the foolish virgins did not have enough time to prepare themselves for stamina; they had used their place of preparation to become a place of comfort, and so they were left out, because they could not finish the race. Champions do not go to sleep when it is time for work—they use their place of comfort to become a place for their assignment. He is one that fulfills all the obligations—he never says the word can't, because he or she believes that all things are possible. A Champion never enters a race to quit—he believes that a winner never quits, and a quitter never wins. He is always in for a win, and he keeps fighting, because he believes in the Champion that is living within.

GOING THE DISTANCE:

Whatever you plan to achieve in life, you will need to have your mind set on going all the way. Life comes with many obstacles, and many oppositions. Just like a race, you will sometimes have to go over some hurdles, and go around the bend before getting back on the straight line that leads to the finishing point. When getting to your final point, you will have to make up your mind to go around those curves, jump over those hurdles, and go through the pain and fatigue. You have to be willing to fight life in order for you to achieve, and come out victorious. Going the distance, you need a mind that is made up, and a mind that is prepared to go all the way. There are people that look at the shortcuts, and the quick route in getting through life. It's like trying to cheat life in getting to your destiny. To learn about real life, and its definition, there is no short cut. Some people choose to become lazy, and would rather beg to survive, while some choose to steal. Some play the lottery, hoping to win the mega-million or Power Ball, and become rich. It then becomes their addiction, which causes some to become broke trying to become rich the easy way. There are some that win, but later they lose it all, because they did not go the distance to understand the meaning of winning and gaining. There are some who win, but then they forget about their souls. Whatever way you choose in going the distance, there will be a cost—however, taking the long route is better in going the distance. It will be worth the cost, rather than taking the shortcuts, or trying to cheat your way through. Taking the short cut in life means that you are not prepared to go the distance, or you are not prepared to fight. Life comes with giving and taking. It is like celebrating Christmas, or having a birthday celebration: some bring gifts while the other receives gifts. Paying the cost in going the distance in life will be appreciated in the end. There are some fathers and some mothers that have given up on their children. Some refuse to pay child support; some refuse to visit their children. They are not ready to go the distance in becoming the mother and father that they were created to be. Jesus said, in His words, "No man, having put his hand to the plough, and looking back, is fit for the kingdom of God." (St. Luke 9:62) Looking back is a sign giving up, and a sign of not going the distance. Imaging going into a fight that is scheduled for fifteen rounds! If you only prepare for an early knock-out in the third round, there is a chance that you won't make it to ten rounds, if the fight goes past three rounds—because you only prepared to go three. This possibly means someone could get stopped in the fight. If your opponent prepared to go fifteen rounds, it means that he did not prepare to get knocked out. The person who prepared to go the distance will eventually be the winner. Don't plan for a quick knock-out; don't plan to take the shortcut; don't plan to cheat your way through; plan to go the distance. You will never know how far you will go, or how much you will accomplish in life, if you are not prepared to go the distant. Don't settle for less; don't sell yourself short; there is more on the inside than you can imagine. All you have to do is dream big, believe it, then step out in faith and do it. Sometimes you will feel like quitting and giving up. The reason you will feel this way is that you are moving to the next level that you thought would be impossible. Moving to the next level is moving beyond your imagination, beyond your feelings. Don't just believe in what you see—expand your belief that there is more beyond what you are seeing. Sometimes you only see the icing on the cake, but there is even more in the cake than just looking at the cake. Notice that, in the life of Joseph (in the Bible), he did not dream about bowing down to his brothers; in his dream, it was his brothers bowing down before him. (Genesis 37:7-9) He went through some setbacks in his life which I could call the hurdles and the curves of life; however, they did not stop him from fulfilling his dream. He was thrown into a pit by his brothers, because they were trying to stop him from fulfilling his dream, as found in verse 24. He was later taken from the pit to become overseers in the house of his master, as described in Genesis 39:2-5. He later suffered a setback, after being framed by his master's wife, and was put into prison, as written in verse 20. But the Lord was with him. Joseph would not give up on his dream, and was willing to go the distance. He kept dreaming, and even dreamed bigger in prison. He was later taken from the prison and became the prince of Egypt (Genesis 41:41-44). All his setbacks and opposition could not stop him from going the distance in reaching his destiny and fulfilling his dream. In going the distance, you have to keep dreaming. Keep fighting; keep trying; keep believing.

A Champion for God:

A Champion for God is one who goes through what I would call "The valley of life" or "The storms of life"—one who meets the requirements of being loyal, faithful, dedicated, upright, and just before God. I look at men that the Bible speaks about, such as Job, David, Jeremiah, Daniel, Shadrach, Meshach, Abednego, Moses, Joseph, Abraham, and Gideon, etc. Those are men that can be considered Champions for God, because their faith has being tested, and their Character was proven. God tried them, and found them worth the cost of becoming Champions, and men who has proven God to be real. When you are a Champion for God, you don't judge the circumstances, or the outcome of life by the external situation. A Champion of God judges life and the external based on the God that lives on the inside. It does not matter what you will face in your valleys, or in your storms. It does not matter the amount of enemies that surround your life. It does not matter the caves or the pits that you might find yourselves in—what really matter is that you have the faith, the courage, and the strength to say, "I can do all things through Christ who strengthen me." (Philippians 4:13) "Greater is He that is in me, than he that is in this world" (1 John 4:4) "You come to me with a spear and a sword, but I come to you in the name of the Lord of Hosts." (1 Samuel 17:45) "What then shall we say to these things? If God is for us, who can be against us?" (Romans 8:31)

Champions for God are those who depend on His word, those who cannot live without His word, and those who know that the only power that they have can only be demonstrated through the word of God. There are many people in this world that are Christians—however, the name *Christian* can be defined as a religion, but one that is ready to live the true life of a Christian must be ready to live a spiritual life. In addition, you must be willing to live a life of faith. This means that your faith must be proven; you must be willing to go through the uncertain, not knowing what the outcome will be. You must be willing to trust God, knowing that He is able to bring you out. The three Hebrew boys in Daniel chapter 3 were considered =Champions because they were willing to go through their fire and, even if God did not show up, they would still not bow down to an image (Daniel 3:17-18). Champions can be defined like David who went up to fight his giant, because he put his faith in God, and knew that God would give him the victory—which God did. Champions are those who did not give up, and persevere like Job. He was stripped of his livestock, family, and lost flesh from his body, even to the point where he was told to curse God and die. "Then said his wife unto him, 'Dost thou still retain him? Dost thou still retain thine integrity? Curse God, and die!'" (Job 2:9 KJV) However, Job remained the Champion, and would prove to the world that when circumstances come to test you, they do not disqualify you from being a Champion. The storms and the fear of life cannot deny or defy you from being the Champion that God called you to be. Rather, it is the Champion in you that defies and denies the fear, the storms, and the so-called giants of life that come to block you from reaching your destiny, and from fulfilling the things that God requires of you to complete. Sometimes a Champion for God will get weak in his or her own strength, and become discouraged and even frustrated. This is because a Champion for God does not fight his or her own battle. He does not rely on his own strength. A Champion will get weak in order to understand that it is not he or she fighting and winning the battle, but it is the Spirit of God that does so. The scripture tells us, "Not by might nor power, but by my Spirit, says the Lord." (Zechariah 4:6) It is the Spirit of God that works in those whom

God chooses to use. It equips us and it enables us to do the impossible in winning the battle—all you have to do is believe in the power of the Spirit of God. The Bible tells us in the gospel of St. John 1, "But as many as received Him, to them gave He power to become sons of God, even to them that believe on His name." (St. John 1:12) He gave power to them that have a Spirit of humility, one who is gentle and humble. It was the apostle, one that I admired as a Champion for God, one who was willing to be bold in the midst of adversities who said these words: "I can do all things through Christ Jesus who strengthens me." (Philippians 4:13) Jesus also said these words: "I can of myself do nothing." St. John 5:30) He wants us to know that we are weak in our own selves, and can do nothing, and are failures without God. Samson was known to be the strongest man that ever lived, yet in his own strength he became weak. He became weak, because the Spirit of God had departed from him (Judges 16:20). Before his death with the Philistines, he had to pray to God to strengthen him: "And Samson called unto the Lord, 'O Lord God, remember me, I pray thee, and strengthen me, I pray thee, only this once, O God, that I may be at once avenged of the Philistines for my two eyes." (Judges 16:28) It was after the Lord strengthened him, that he broke down the pillar of the temple, killing many of the Philistines, even killing himself in the process (Judges 16:29-30). Gideon was one who I also admired as a Champion for God. After God told Gideon to go and save Israel from the Midianites, he did not see himself as qualified, because of his status. "And he said unto him, 'Oh my Lord, wherewith shall I save Israel? Behold, my family is poor in Manasseh, and I am the least in my father's house." (Judges 6:15) Although Gideon was not qualified, God chose him to go up against an army that was much more powerful at that time. In addition, Gideon did have too many people in the eyes of God to go up against the Midianites army, although the Amalekites did join together with the Midianites (verse 3) which made it more difficult for Israel to have a chance. God decreased Gideon's army to a number of 300 people, which did make it seem impossible to go against an army of over two million people (Judges 7:7). God did this so that the people of Israel would not think that they did it themselves, as told in verse 2. Jehoshaphat was known to be a humble King, with a small army. He was confronted by the Moabites, and the Ammonites for battle (2 Chronicles 20). According to verse 12, Jehoshaphat had neither might nor power to fight against these two armies—but God sent a word to let Jehoshaphat know that he would not need to fight. "Ye shall not need to fight in this battle: set yourselves, stand ye still, and see the salvation of the Lord with you, O Judah and Jerusalem; fear not, nor be dismayed; tomorrow go up against them, for the Lord will be with you." (2. Chronicles 20:17). A person who desired to be a Champion for God must acknowledge his or her own weakness—you can do nothing on your own without God. In addition, you must seek God in the areas where you are struggling. You need spiritual strength, and you also need spiritual wisdom to do the will of God. The Bible tells us in the book of James, "If any of you lack wisdom, let him ask God, who giveth to all men liberally, and upbraideth not; and it shall be given him." (James 1:5 KJV). A Champion for God must expect some kind of challenge on a spiritual level; this means that you don't run or remain frustrated in your time of challenge—you need to embrace the challenge. There are people who fail the test because of their challenges, and choose to run from them. Wherever you are weak as a Champion for God that is where you will be most challenged. This is also the area where the Devil will challenge you the most. In addition, God's desire is for you to use your faith to conquer your weakness. This is the reason why James also tells the reader, "Knowing that the trying of your faith worketh patience. But let patience have her perfect work, that ye may be perfect and entire, wanting nothing," (James 1:3-4 KJV) I remembered in my young days of boxing, one of my weaknesses was throwing my right hand, but stretching while keeping my feet too far apart. I often would do so when trying to take my opponent out, after he was in trouble. The danger in doing so was, if my opponent would evade the punch, it would be easy for my opponent to counter me, because I would have less time moving away when my feet were too far apart. My trainer let me know that I could still finish my opponent off without trying to load up and leaving myself open. To prevent this, he then would strap an elastic band to both ankles so that I only could stretch my feet to the width of the elastic band. After finding out my weakness, I would do my road work with the elastic band on both ankles, making sure that my weakness would be resolved, and that I would never leave myself open while trying to go for the knock out. It is the same way in doing God's work,—you must continue to pray to God for wisdom, and try to correct your own weakness. Although a Champion could be behind on the score card, or even be in the last bottom, that does not stop him or her from making it to the top. This is where you are able to prove your faith and your character; the Champion in you will define who you really are. The bottom or the last back of the line can be viewed as your training ground, or the place that will prove your definition of character, which will define who you really are. Take an example from the life of Joseph—he was one that can be admired as a Champion for God. He was first thrown into a pit by his brothers, as written about in Genesis 37:24. He had a setback and was thrown into prison (Genesis 39:20). However, his pit and his prison did not stop him from being the Champion that God called him to be; the pit and the prison could not hinder him from becoming the prince of Egypt that he later became, and those places were just used by God to become his place of preparation. It was through his prison where he developed his humility and his Character. The Bible does not give any indication of high school or college where Joseph went to study. Champions for God do not receive qualifications because of their degree or status; they don't earn titles as Champions because of names, or fame. They become Champions because their character was tested and was proven. You must be willing to endure, to persevere, and to show your faith, to stand in the face of adversities, and prove God. A Champion for God will not compromise, even if God does not show up; he or she will prove the impossible to become possible, the incredible to become credible. He or she does not see the battle as those who are losers. Losers tell themselves that they can't, while Champions for God tells themselves, *I can, I will, I believe, it is possible.* Losers walk by sight, and see the natural, while Champions walk by faith, and see the supernatural. A loser sees him or herself as a caterpillar, always crawling on its belly, or one who walks with his or her head down, while Champions for God always see him or herself as a butterfly, flying high in the sky. Champions for God do not stop, because he or she has a place, and a destiny to reach.

CHAMPIONS OF HOPE:

To be the Champion that God called you to be, you must see yourself as a Champion of hope. It is very sad to see a child of God walking with his or her head held down. You don't need to look down, or walk with your head held down when you are a child of God. In addition, you don't need to walk with a sad countenance—walk with your head held high, with your spirit lifted high, to let the Devil know that you are walking in victory. The Devil's desire is for you to feel as if you are walking, living, and fighting a losing battle. You need to know that if you are in the army of God, you are on the winning side. This makes you a Champion, one who walks in confidence, one who walks with a word of encouragement. You must know that you can encourage yourself, even when the battle does not seem to be in your favor. David was one to be admired as a Champion of hope. The Bible tells us in 1 Samuel chapter 30 that, after David reached home, the Amalekites had invaded his territory (which was known as Ziklag). His wives and livestock were all taken away, and the city of Ziklag was smitten, and burned with fire (verse 2-3). This was like trying to swallow a pill without water. David now seemed to be in a hopeless situation. In verse 4, it says "Then David and the people that were with him lifted up their voice and wept, until they had no more power to weep." (1 Samuel 30:4 KJV). The verse tells us that there was no more power in David to weep, which this brings question:

How do you find strength in your time of weakness? How do you find hope, when everything seems to be hopeless? Of course, in the life of a Champion for God, you will sometimes find yourself at a place of weakness. Sometimes you will ask God what to do, when you don't really know what to do. This is where God wants you to put your hope, your trust, and your faith in trusting Him, knowing that God is using your challenges and difficulties to prepare you, and that in the end, you will give Him all the glory. A child who God chooses to become a Champion will not always walk in the park like a bed of roses, or as if walking on cotton. To be the Champion that God called you to be comes with much turmoil; you will face many difficulties, heartache and hardship. Sometimes it will feel as if you are fighting on your own. You will not be exempt from trouble. Job, who went through tremendous suffering, said these words: "Man that is born of a woman is of few days, and full of trouble" (Job 14:1 KJV). David had come to understand that you don't have to go out looking for trouble, because trouble will sometimes show up at your front door. "And David was greatly distressed, for the people spoke of stoning him, because the soul of all the people was grieved, every man for his sons and for his daughters; but David encouraged himself in the Lord his God." (1 Samuel 30:6 KJV). David was left alone to prove himself, and the Champion that he was for God. He was left to deal with the people's pain, and to bear their burden. A Champion must know how to deal with pain, and how it feels to be mentally, physically, and emotionally hurt. He or she is not one that runs away from the responsibility. Although David was feeling distressed, he did not give up, or walk with his head held down, he did not show any form of attitude because of the way he was feeling. In addition, he did not complain, or show any form of retaliation, though he was frustrated. He rather turned to the God in whom he put his trust. What do you do, when you don't know what to do? What do you do when you are too weak to fight, and are feeling discouraged in your own strength?" David gave us a perfect example—he encouraged himself in the Lord (verse 6). This speaks about the character, and the heart of a Champion. He is one that does not easily change or move because of the circumstances that surrounds his or her situation. Hope and faith in God will turn the situation and circum-stances into his or her favor. The ways in which a Champion deals with opposition will give people hope. It was later in the chapter where David enquired of God his next step in pursuing his enemies. God then responded to David that he should pursue, and that surely he would recover (verse 8). Everything was, at one point, taken from David, in that he recovered more than what was taken, including his wives; he was then able to share from the recovery, as told in verse 26. This was because David put his faith, his trust and his hope in God, and proved that he was a Champion of hope.

THE CHARACTER OF A CHAMPION:

Although a Champion may get knocked down or have a setback, he is one that takes his setbacks and knock-downs with pride; he learns from his knock-downs and setbacks, using those mistakes to correct and redeem him or herself. A Champion takes pride in humility. He is one that has confidence on the inside, although it may look difficult from an outside appearance. David did not fit the task of fighting Goliath; he did not look qualified, because he was just a youth, while the giant was a man of war from his days of youth (1 Samuel 17:33). The giant Goliath judged David because of his size and the weapon that David chose to fight him (1 Samuel 17:42-43), but David's confidence was in the Lord. A true Champion does not rely on his own strength, but his or her confidence is in the Lord God. David's mind was already made up to face the giant, although fear was standing in his way. Although King Saul tried to put fear in him, he proved to the King that "God did not give him a Spirit of fear, but of power, of love, and of a sound mind." (2 Timothy 1:7) I remember as a young fighter, and a Champion for Jamaica, that I was one who did not fit the description of a fighter, I did not have the muscles— the only thing that I knew that I had was my determination. I was not known to be a bully—I was the one who would get picked on in school, until most of the students from school were my friends. You don't show your strength and power by becoming a bully—you do this by being humble, and by showing compassion and humility. He finds the reason why he went down the first time, and works on that mistake so that he can come back stronger. Champions do not try to rush, or hurry—he or she is one that shows patience, and takes discipline as a learning process, until he learns to become a disciple. A true Champion does not rush to get off the canvas, if he or she gets knocked down, or when there is some kind of delay or setback—he or she takes his recovery slowly. In, addition he takes recovery with humility. Humility is a place where God takes true Champions to keep them humble, and when they leave that place of humility, they will now be on their way to become great. Many so-called Champions went down the second time harder than the first, because the recovery from the first knock-down was not complete. The real Champion asked him or herself the question, *What went wrong? How do I correct this mistake? What did I learn from my knock-down?* Your knock-down helps you to do better, because it is not a place for a champion to find him or herself. It also helps you to understand where you came from, what you came through, and where you need to be. In addition, he makes you want to work harder to keep your title as a Champion, because it is not an easy road getting there. I remember that twice I made it from off the canvas to fight back, then won the outcome. In my fourth professional fight, I got knocked down, because I took my eyes off my opponent. My mind went somewhere else, until I found myself getting up to my feet. This was like a wakeup call for me; after my knock-down, I get up then fight back and won the match. I also mention in my first book about getting knocked down in Puerto Rico, and how I was given the option to fight again. Some of my teammates tried to stop me, because they were in fear for me. However, it was not an option to take a loss and get comfortable when I had the chance to fight again, and to redeem myself. I was able to correct my mistake, and prove to the judges, my teammates, and the boxing fans that there is a Champion in me.

People will never see or admire your characteristics until they have seen your labor and the many hardships that you are willing to face while you still come out victorious. To have some form of definition in your life, you must first go through something to define those definitions and characteristics. This is what will give people the confidence to believe in the real person that lives in you. This was the reason why Thomas believed that it was the Lord Jesus, after

Jesus was raised from the dead. Thomas said, "Except I shall see in his hands the print of the nails, and thrust my hand in his side, I will not believe." (St. John 20: 25) The nail's print proves, or defines, that Jesus Christ was on the cross. So it is with a Champion; you will never know the Champion that is inside of you before facing the storm, obstacles, and all the things that will come to prove you. As I pictured the young shepherd boy whose name was David, who went out to face his giant at an early age, it makes me reflect upon my own life. I was seventeen years old when I decided to started life on my own. I did not have another option as to whether I should start life at a very young age—that was my only option. I remember working as the only brother of eight, with two sisters, trying to do the very best that I could to support my family. I was working two jobs, and was also boxing at the same time. One of my early tragedies happened after my little home got burned down. I had to live with a friend for some time until I could have a home for myself. Five years later, a hurricane came through and swept my home away. I did not understand why I had to go through these set-backs at such an early age—however, I was a very determined person, one who was willing to fight, and to do whatever it took to make it in life. Five months later, I joined a boxing gym. This was my only option. I was put to the test, or in other words, I was force to prove myself as a Champion, to bring out the true Champion that was in me. Your knock-downs in life help you to understand that you don't have to get too comfortable. The clock is ticking—you only have eight seconds to get back on your feet, or else you will be counted out.

FACING YOUR GIANT OF FEAR:

One of the most difficult things that you must get through in life before reaching your next level is facing your Giant of fear. Your Giant of fear can be described as the things that will come to oppose you in life. Whatever it is that that your desires are to fulfill or accomplish, there will be some kind of obstacle that can be looked at as a Giant, to bring fear. Going back to school after twenty-five years to pursue your education can be seen as a Giant of fear. There will be some kind of challenges that you will face. You will have to sacrifice time for studying; you will also struggle during your studying. You will be worrying at times about paying your school loans, if you are required to do so. Getting into the ring to win a title that you trained very hard for comes with a fear of facing your Giant. Going on the track to compete for a gold medal that you anxiously anticipate comes with the fear of facing your Giant. This shows, before your Giant comes, that your fear will come. The question that is to be asked is, *why?* Your Giant is not real; you can easily get past your Giant. The weapon of your Giant is your fear. The Devil always puts on this image which is just "False Evidence Appearing Real." If you fail to rely on the word of God, you will allow fear to go before your faith. This is why the word of God tells us, "For God hath not given us a Spirit of fear; but of power, and of love, and of a sound mind." (2 Timothy 1:7) God's desire for us is to use our God-given Spirit to walk, and our eyes of faith to see. Of course the word of God is Spirit, as written in Ephesians 6:17. For you to understand the things of God, and to know where you are going, you must see with our eyes of faith, and not with the natural eyes. (2 Corinthians 5:7) Whenever you decide to climb a tall mountain, even before starting, the image will come to your mind. Although it could be a walk in the park for someone that is in great shape, the first impression is its image. The Devil always presents an image to bring fear to the mind. The image of fear comes to blind your eyes of faith. In addition, it comes to bring doubt to your belief. This is why Jesus told his disciples, "Have faith in God." (St. Mark 11:22) "For verily I say unto you, that whosoever shall say unto this mountain, be thou removed, and be thou cast into the sea; and shall not doubt in his heart, but shall believe that those things which he saith shall come to pass, he shall have whatsoever he saith." (St. Mark 11:23) Your mountains and your giants are not your real enemy—your fear is the real enemy. Your weapon is the word of God, which is the Spirit in you. I have often wondered why God allowed difficulties and challenges to come to the ones that He loved—why they often come my way. I did not and could not know that I have the strength and the courage to overcome them until after I came out in triumph. David could not and would not know the King that was on the inside until he defeated his Giant. All the great Champions in sports, like Tiger Woods, Michael Phelps, Evander Holyfield, and Usain Bolt could not have become Champions before facing the crowd, and their Giants of fear that come to oppose them. When I decided to leave Jamaica to live in the United States, I did not have much money in my pocket, and did not have any family members in Boston. My father and mother were all worried, as they wondered about my resources. My father tried very hard to discourage me; I remember hearing him saying to me, "Paul, how are you going to make it in Boston? You don't have any money in your pocket, and you don't have any family over there !" I looked at my father and said, "Papa, I am stepping out in faith, and God will make a way for me." Before I would be heading to the airport, I had to face the fear to my destiny. The Devil will always use an image of "false evidence appearing real." It is an image to wrestle the mind, to stop you, to disturb you, and to cause you to worry about the outcome. He will do this to put the Champion to sleep on the inside of you. The only thing that stands in the way of a Champion is an image of fear. A real Champion is one that believes in him or herself; he does not look at the external situation, because he believes in him or herself. Why does the Devil send fear before the Giant? Fear comes to stop you from taking down your Giant, and it comes to stop you from bringing the Champion out. However, if you believe in the Champion in you, fear cannot stop you, it cannot defeat you. The only person that can defeat a Champion is a Champion, and that is the one inside of you. Where does the Champion live in you? This, I believe, is a good question to answer, because the Champion in you must be in your belief, which means, the Champion lives in your mind. Either you believe that you can, or you can't. This can be understood from the Israelites' experience in their wilderness. Why did they fail on the promises of God? It was all in their mind. They were lacking in their knowledge, wisdom, understanding, and their belief in the word of God. God had pre-pared and reserved some lands to give the people of Israel, when God told Moses, "Send thou men, that they may search the land of Canaan, which I give unto the children of Israel; of every tribe of their fathers shall ye send a man, every one a ruler among them." (Numbers 13:2) However, before they could possess what God gave unto them, they had to first believe in the word of God, and second, they would have to trust God with their eyes of faith, which would get them ready to pass their fear, and defeat their Giants which were standing in their way (Numbers 13:28). Your Giant of fear comes to deprive, and to deny you from the things that God prepared for you to have. According to Numbers 13:27, the land was good, flowing with milk and honey. Although the land was good, verse 32 tells the readers that the people came up with their own evil report: that the land had eaten up the inhabitant thereof. In other words, they told a lie that the land was not good. Their fear began to mess with their minds, saying that they didn't see things the way God presented them. Their fear forced them to lie, and to sin before God. Fear is something that sets you up to fail; it allows you to see the negative, rather than the positive. Not only does fear mess with your mind, but it also messes with your speech. It blocks you from speaking the truth, and from seeing things from a positive perspective. "And they returned from searching the land after forty days." (Numbers 13:25) Imagine forty days—forty is the number of completion. But because of their fear, they could not complete their assignment; instead their fear only caused them to wander in their wilderness, going around in circles. They gave up, then came back all looking defeated, as they thought they were. Their fear had now forced them to bring back an excuse, and the reason why they could not claim the land, and so they brought back an evil report. They came back with fear to tell Moses, Aaron, and the congregation in verse 26. You must be careful about the people that you keep on your team—some do not come to win, and they only come to bring fear, because they don't believe in themselves. If they fail to believe in themselves, they will also fail to believe in you. This was the reason why Jesus had to get rid of some fake followers on his way to the house of Jairus, when he said, "Why make ye this ado, and weep? The damsel is not dead, but sleepeth." (St. Mark 5:39) Of course, Jesus knew that the child was dead—however he also knew that they were fake crying, this was why they began laughing as if the Lord did not know. This was why he put them out in St Mark chapter 5 verse 40, and brought in his three disciples, Peter, James, and John, along with the mother and father. You've got to know who to trust, and also who to believe on your team. Some of these Israelites made up their own negative report to bring fear to the people. They believed a word from the enemy, rather than the word of God. "And they went and came to Moses, and to Aaron, and to all the congregation of the children of Israel, unto the wilderness of Paran, to Kadesh, and brought back words unto them, and to all the congregation, and showed them the fruits of the land." (Numbers 13:26) Although they brought back a report concerning the blessings of the land, their signature was a sign of fear that stopped their destiny. "Nevertheless, the people be strong that dwell in the land, and the cities are walled, and very great; and moreover we saw the children of Anak there." (Numbers 13:28) The Israelites did not know how strong the people were, because they did not prove their strength; they only believed in what they saw with their natural eyes. Their fear failed them from believing and receiving the things that God reserved for them to achieve. The Devil still used this image of fear to battle one's belief, to isolate and to create a stumbling block in the mind of every child of God, preventing them from reaching the promises and the things that God had ordained for their lives.

Overcoming the Battle: For you to overcome the battle of fear, you must first believe in the word of God that you are who God says you are. The Lord tells us in His word, "And the Lord shall make thee the head, and not the tail; and thou shalt be above only, and shall be beneath; if that thou hearken unto the commandments of the Lord thy God, which I command thee this day, to observe and to do them." (Deuteronomy 28:13) In addition, "Ye are of God, little children, and have overcome them, because greater is he that is in you than he that is in the world." (1 John 4:4) To translate Deuteronomy 28, it bestowed blessings to those who hearken to the word of God, and believe in His commandments. In 1 John 4, it begins with one's beliefs. Don't believe in every spirit—you should first try them, and develop spiritual discernment, because there are many evil spirits that have gone out into this world—spirits that the Devil uses to deprive one's blessings. They come to steal, to kill, and to destroy—see St. John 10:10. To bring the Champion out of you, and to be the person that God called you to be, you must first step out of your fear, and step out on faith. Second, you must use the word of God as your weapon to defeat your fear and the giant that stands in your way. There are many people who have run away from their God-given assignment—people who gave up on their destiny because of fear. David gave us an example about facing his Giant of fear. He refused the weapons of men, and rather stepped out in the word of God. He told King Saul that it was God who delivered him out of the paws of the lion, and the bear, and the uncircumcised Philistine shall be as one of them. 1 Samuel 17:37. In addition, in approaching the giant Goliath, he addressed the Lord as his deliverer, and said that God would deliver him, that all the assembly would know that the Lord does not save with sword and spear, for the battle is the Lord's, as written in verse 47. This chapter is to let you know that in everything, you must accomplish, there will be some kind of obstacle that you must overcome. However, if you place the word of God as your direction, you will be able to overcome every challenge that will come your way. The difference between David and the children of Israel is that David went with the word of God, while the children of Israel went up in fear.

FIGHTING AGAINST MY OWN FEAR:

Many athletes that compete competes with fear in the mind. Fear is something that triggered the mind, and your belief. It is something that always tells you it is impossible to get done. Fear is something that sets you up for failure. In the sport of boxing, I have witnessed many fighters, including some whom I fought and beat in previous fights, enter the boxing ring with the image of fear in their eyes. It happened at one of the games where I was fighting for Jamaica—a team-mate of mine who lost to a Cuban fighter in one of the previous games entered the ring to meet the same Cuban, with the fear of his past. Whenever there is a game like the Olympics, the Central-American and Caribbean games, the Pan-American games, or the Guadeloupe games, the Cuban fighters are known to be very good boxers, and are the ones that walk away with the most medals. Most fighters from other Caribbean islands enter the ring in fear when fighting a Cuban fighter. No one hopes to meet a Cuban fighter in the first fight, because there is a risk of getting eliminated from the game without winning a medal. Often, the trainers are the ones that pick the name from a bucket with all the names of the fighters, like raffling. Whoever the trainers pick during the raffle, his fighter will fight that opponent. At the time of the drawing, all eyes were on my team-mate, because he was hoping that our trainer would not pick the name of the Cuban that beat him in the Pan American games. Our trainer picked the name from the bucket and looked at the name,, then turned to my team-mate and said, "You are fighting the same Cuban—the one who knocked you out in the Pan American games." My team-mate then put his hands on his head and said, "Why me Lord? Why me?" This is the same way the Devil works in the dark—as my trainer reminded my team-mate about the loss of his past, it is the same way in which the Devil brings back your past, because his desire is to remind you of the times when you were knocked out, or when you were a victim. He want you to see yourself as who you were, rather than who you are. This is the reason why many athletes, or even people who come through some kind of tragedy, walk with this image, which causes them to see themselves fighting against their own fear. At the fight that night, my team-mate was in the fear of his life. As soon as the bell rang, he went out to meet the Cuban, and he was on his back when the first punch of the fight was thrown. While our trainer was taking off the gloves, he came to himself then asked the trainer, "What are you doing" The trainer then said, "The fight is over, you got knocked out. He then said, "What! I did not feel anything." Many of my team-mates thought it was funny. I now understand that it was his own fear that set him up to fail. I have learned from going into the boxing ring and looking into the eyes of my opponent before the fight takes place that each fighter looks for a sign of fear. I have seen many fighters who went inside the ring to fight Mike Tyson who seemed to lose the fight before the bell rang. The reason is because they lost in fighting their own fear. The only person to beat you is yourself. It is just like the children of Israel who denied themselves from the land that God gave them, because of fear. To win the battle of fear, you need to have confidence in yourself; believe in yourself, believe in the Champion in you, and walk in faith with the word of God as your weapon.

THE THOUGHT OF A CHAMPION:

Your thoughts are your decisions; they decide what you will do, and what you will become. Whoever you are, that's who you thought of becoming. The person who becomes famous and popular did not just become famous and popular overnight—it was a thought that was already registered in the person's mind. The thought of a Champion is powerful; it can be used as a phrase, saying, "I believe in myself." If you know that there is a Champion in you, then you will believe in the Champion that lives on the inside. You have to believe that there is power in your thoughts, because your beliefs tell who you are. Everything in life begins with a thought. If you think like a Champion, there is a Champion in you, because it was already in your mind. The Bible tells us, "As a man thinketh in his heart, so is he." (Proverbs 23:7). The thought of a Champion proves his or her character, because, "Your thought will become your word, your word will become your action, and your action will becomes your character." Whatever you are thinking on the inside one day will become a reality. Before one commits a crime, the person has to think about it. This is the reason the Bible tells the reader, "That whosoever looketh on a woman to lust after her hath committed adultery with her already in his heart." (St. Matthew 5:28). The thought of a Champion proves that he or she believes in himself. Whatever you think, that's what you will do; whatever you do, that's who you are. If I had the mind to become a barber, sooner or later I will start cutting hair, because it was already in my thoughts. Some of the things that I thought about on a daily basis, I went to sleep and dreamt about them. Your thoughts are so powerful that they can cause you to dream. If you forget the thought that you dream, you can rely on your thought to remind you, because it will always be there. If you think like a Champion, then dream about it; it is impossible to forget, because that's who you are on the inside. If you continue hanging around cars, and hanging around mechanics, it's possible that you will become a mechanic, because it was already in your thoughts. The devil's plan is to mess with your thoughts; he does not want you to think positively, or constructively. Your thoughts can help you to possess wealth, and can bring motivation through words. A pilot would not be able to fly a plane if he never thought of becoming a pilot. You can miss out on the things that could make you become successful, because you did not think about them. Whenever someone takes illegal drugs and messes with his or her mind and thoughts, he cannot think positively. Some people's pain and afflictions have caused them to be depressed in their thoughts. This is the plan of the Devil to stop them from believing in the person God created them to be. This is why he will bring fear to your mind, and to stop you from reaching your destiny. A Champion's thoughts will defeat his or her fear, because a Champion is a winner, and to have fear will make you a loser. If you have the thoughts of a Champion, you will live a life of victory, because of your beliefs. If you believe that you can win, then you are already a winner on the inside. The thought of a Champion is another way of saying, "I have power in my beliefs." Whatever you believe makes you the person you are. If a person is a double-minded person, that's who he or she will be, because their mind is unstable in every way, as written in James 1:8. Such a person does not know what to believe, and will change his or her beliefs easily. You cannot change who you are, if that's who you are. Even a person with a double mind cannot change his ways, because that's who the person is. The only way to change is if the person changes his beliefs—changing from being a double-minded to a single-minded person. It begins with a thought. Someone may try to get you upset by calling you a nickname—however, as long as you don't accept or believe, they cannot hurt your feelings. It's just like someone calling you on a long-distance phone call, and having to go through an operator: unless you accept the charges, the call cannot go through. You cannot be responsible for the call or the charges. It is the same with your thoughts and beliefs. The thoughts of a Champion will bring out the Champion on the inside. An undisputed Champion does not just enter the ring to win another Championship, or enter a race to be a winner. Before he or she enters the ring or the race, it was already in their thoughts to be a Champion, and a winner. Some people accept failures, because they did not believe in themselves that they could become victorious. You could be walking the street without having a dime in your pocket and without money in your account, and still believe that you are a rich person. If your thoughts make you a millionaire, that's the character people will see on the outside. Although they may not know how much money is in your pocket or your account, they will only see you for who you are on the outside, because those are your thoughts and beliefs on the inside. To beat a Champion, you will have to find some ways to get into his thoughts to change it, which is impossible, because to beat a Champion, you have to be the Champion. Imagine two Champions playing chess! One will have to be able to outsmart the other. However, it is impossible to figure out the thoughts of a Champion. He may not look like the way he thinks: he may not act like the way he thinks, however he is always ahead in his thoughts. He always has a way and a plan to win, because that's who he is. This also means there can only be one undisputed Champion. In addition, a Champion is second to none, because he or she stands alone.

THE MIND OF A CHAMPION:

The mind of a Champion is a mind that is made up for greatness; he or she will go the extra mile, or will believe in their mind to do the impossible—because their mind is already made up. They will make sure that the job get done, without wavering, or leaving business unfinished. Champions are those who see and believes in the outcome without making any form of excuse. This means that a Champion is not one that compromises, but is willing to bind up the gap. He or she will not team up with bystanders, or spectators on the sidewalk, because some only show up to see the battle, while some run away from the battle: In addition, some show up to see the Champion. A Champion is one that runs towards the battle with confidence. A Champion makes room for him or herself to get to the battle, with a mind to win, and a heart that is determined. You cannot pay a Champion to become a Champion, because the Champion is already on the inside. Before you put the gloves on your hands, before you put the helmet on, before you put the shorts on, and go on the track or in the ring, you are already a Champion. You may have suffered a knock-down, have some kind of setback— however, you were already a Champion even before your setbacks or your comebacks. Before you were born, you were a Champion just waiting to come forth. All you need is the heart that is determined, and the mind that is made up to go through the preparation before seeing the person that lives in you. The prophet Jeremiah was already a prophet ordained by God to speak to a nation, even before he was conceived in the womb. Jeremiah did not see himself as a prophet, because he was just a little boy when the Lord called him, as written in Jeremiah 1:5. God knows that our tasks would and will be difficult, and that's why He prepares us for our destiny. All we need to do is believe in the word of God, and believe in ourselves, and face the challenges for preparation. God told the Prophet Jeremiah, "Before I formed thee in the belly I know thee; and before thou camest forth out of the womb I sanctified thee, and I ordained thee a prophet unto the nations." (Jeremiah 1:5 KJV). Even before Jeremiah faced his challenge, he was already set aside to be a prophet, and was equipped and ready to face it. The problem was that he did not know, and even when God told him, he tried to make excuses, which means that his mind was not made up to believe. Before you faced your first test or challenge, the Champion was already in you. Imagine if God did not let Jeremiah know that he was already ordained and sanctified in the womb to be a prophet! He would never know or believe in the prophet that was within him; this was the reason he came up with his own excuse. Even if nobody tells you about the Champion that is in you, you still need to believe in yourself. After believing in yourself, you must be confident of the Champion in you. Whatever you believe, you must believe that it will happen. Don't let people deny the Champion in you; don't let people decide your destiny, because you have the power from within. The word of God tells us, "But as many as received him, to them gave ye power to become sons of God, even to them that believe on his name." (St. John 1:12KJV). So clearly you can see here that the scripture tells us that those who receive power receive it through their beliefs, by believing in Jesus Christ, the Son of God. Of course the real Champion of life is a Champion for God. To become a Champion for God, you must first believe in God, and then believe in the person that God created you to be, and that is the Champion in you. A true Champion is always ready for action, and never lets failure becomes his or her option. He will never compromise, and will never give in, and is always looking for a way to become a winner. In addition, he or she refuses to lose. Losers see the negative, without a way out, while a Champion sees the positive, and a way to work it out. This was the reason why the children of Israel saw themselves as grasshoppers before the giant, and could not claim the land that God gave unto them, as written in Numbers 13:28 and 33. The losers saw the negative, but Caleb saw the positive. "And Caleb stilled the people before Moses, and said, 'Let us go up at once, and possess it, for we are well able to overcome it." (Numbers 13:30KJV) In addition, the army of King Saul saw the Philistine Goliath as a giant that caused them to flee (1 Samuel 17:24-25), but David saw him as an uncircumcised Philistine. "For who is this uncircumcised Philistine, that he should defy the armies of the living God?" (1 Samuel 17:26 KJV). The difference between a Champion and a loser is that a loser will say that it is impossible, while a Champion says, "All things are possible." A loser doesn't have a passion for redemption, while a Champion has a passion and a vision. This means that a loser keeps looking backward, while a Champion is always looking forward. A loser always look in the rear-view mirror, while a Champion keeps looking forward, never to look backward. A Champion always stays on top, while a loser always stay in the back. If you desire to become a Champion, you cannot hang around losers, because losers will try to discourage you—they believe that "False evidence appears real," which is a saying known by the acronym "F.E.A.R." Losers will pretend to be with you until the giant of their lives shows up. This is when you will know that you are on your own, and will have to bring the Champion out to help you. It happened once in school when I decided to defend a friend of mine who got himself in a fight. It happened that the battle became very intense—however, the friend that I tried to defend got scared and run away, leaving me to fight on my own. I did not know that he ran away until after the fight was calm. I tried to look for him, but he could not be found, and that was when I knew he had disappeared. The next day I asked him, "Why did you run away when I tried to defend you?" He told me that he ran away because there were too many guys, and he was in fear of getting hurt. A loser is a person who thinks selfishly—he or she does not care about the other person

in their surroundings. Whenever you meet a person who think nega-
tively who refuses to push him or herself to go further in life, don't
hang around such person, their desire is to push you backward. They
don't have the heart and the mind to climb, to exhale, to succeed, or
to become Champions. There are people who are willing to settle
for second place, or third place—they are just in the game to get a
medal, to be a contender, or to get a few dollars more. However a
Champion does not compete just to win a trophy—he or she does
not compete just to be in the race, or for a payday. A Champion is
always in it to win it. He or she is one that is prepared to bring out
the best, and nothing less. A Champion will do or die. Second place
is not an option; ninety-nine-and-a-half percent will not be enough
in the eyes of a Champion. A Champion's goal is one hundred
percent. If he receives ninety-nine percent, he will not be satisfied,
and will do whatever it takes—and will even do extra to make up
the one percent. In 1992, while fighting in San Juan Puerto-Rico, I
was competing for the Negril Boxing club (which was the Champion
Boxing Gym for Jamaica). Although I had to fight the same day after
landing in Puerto-Rico, I went inside the ring with confidence,
because I did believed in the Champion that I am, knowing that I
was the better boxer. However, I began trading punch with my
opponent who was much shorter in stature than I was. In addition,
my opponent was known to be a brawler, or a slug fist fighter.
Although he was the shorter fighter, it did seem as if I was getting
the best of him, so I decided to go for a knock-out. As I was trading
punches with my opponent, I got caught on my chin, then went
down to the canvas. I was in a shock as I jumped back to my feet. It
happened that I stumbled after getting to my feet, which forced the
referee to stop the fight without giving the eight count ruling. This
then forced the boxing authorities (who were like the judges), the
boxing doctor, and the boxing commissioner to decide the outcome
of the fight. The fight was then ruled as a premature stoppage, which
means, it had stopped too early without giving the option for recovery. This was when the option was given that I could fight the same
opponent the next night. Many of my team-mates, including my
boxing coach, thought that it was very risky for me to take the fight

the next night, after being knocked down the night before. My team-mates tried to plead with me saying, "Machine Gun, don't take the fight, that kid is a very hard puncher." But I refused to be a loser, and would not accept their option. I remember saying to them, "That kid cannot beat me, he got lucky when he caught me on the chin." They were telling me that my opponent was a dangerous puncher, but I turned their fear into my faith; I let them know that I was the one to be fear, because I was the most dangerous puncher. On that night going into the ring, I could see their fear in the eyes of my team-mates, but I was willing to show them the fighter and the Champion in me. In the rematch, I was on my toes, boxing, jabbing, and dancing. I did not give my opponent a chance to get close to me as I cruised to victory. That night in San Juan Puerto-Rico, I learned that failure is not an option. No one can tell you that you are a loser, or can make you become a loser, unless you believe you are. You have to see yourself as a winner in your mind. If you have a mind that says *I am a winner,* then you will be on your way to become a Champion. To prove that you are a Champion, you will have to step out of your fear, and step out on your faith. You have to see yourself as bigger than your mountain, bigger than the so-called giant, and bigger than everything that will try to oppose you. In addition, you will need a mind that says, "I am a winner, I am a Champion, and I refuse to lose." This will defy the odds, the jeers and critics, and prove to those that are losers that winning is possible if you believe in yourself. My knock-down helped me to understand that failures are not to be accepted—they only gives you the ability to improve your performance, and to do better in life.

BELIEVE IN YOURSELF:

One of the great Champions of all time who also called *himself* the greatest was Muhammad Ali. He fought "Smoking" Joe Frazer three times, and also Ken Norton three times. Muhammad Ali lost the first fight to both fighters, but he went back and redeemed himself to both fighters in the next two fights. He learned from the previous fights, then made his comeback after his setbacks, and redeemed himself, which leaves a legacy as one of the greatest of all time. A trainer does not make a Champion—a Champion is already a Champion even before a meeting with the trainer. The trainer is there to correct the mistakes and the weakness in a Champion. Although the trainer is there to help the Champion, that does not stop the Champion from believing in himself. It is possible for a Champion not to believe in a trainer. It is also possible that the trainer might not believe in what the Champion does or says, because some trainers think that they are the ones who make Champions. However, it is not about the trainer's belief—it is about the Champion believing in his or herself. One of boxing's heavyweight and top fighters was known to be Ken Norton. Earlier I mentioned that he fought Muhammad Ali three times, won the first, and lost the other two fights. In the first fight, he broke Muhammad Ali's jaw, which happened on March 31, 1973. However, Muhammad Ali redeemed himself when he came back to beat Ken Norton twice in their rematches. Although the confident

Ali won the text two fights, Ken Norton, along with some boxing fans, thoughts were that the decisions were controversial. Although Ken Norton lost the second and third fights, he thought that he lost the third fight to Ali because of listening to his trainer rather than doing what he knew and did best. In an interview, Norton said that his last fight with Ali was his best. He said, "I would say that the one I fought the best was the last one at Yankee Stadium. After fifteen rounds, I was not tired, and felt I could've fought fifteen more". Ken Norton was asked which fight he believed Ali fought the best (out of three) and Norton replied, "Would say the second." Again, he was asked which one of the three fights that he thought was the closest: Norton replied, "I would say the second." It sounds fair for Ken Norton to say that Muhammad Ali fought the best in the second fight, and that it was the closest. Although it was a grilling, a thrilling, and intense battle, Ken Norton believed that Muhammad Ali won because of the final round. In addition, he said, "Ali was bigger than boxing at the time." What really convinced me in Ken Norton's interview, in regards to believing in the Champion in you, was Norton's statement concerning the third fight with Ali. He believed that the reason for him losing the fight was taking heed to his trainer, rather than believing in himself. These were the words of Ken Norton in an interview: "I was told by my trainer at the time which was Bill Slayton that I was ahead on points. He said, "Don't go out and get cut, don't go out and get hurt, just go out and control the round and watch yourself and be careful." I went out and thought I did enough to have a draw in that round." Ken was asked, "If you could fight that round again, how would you fight it?" Ken replied," I would fight it like I fought the other fourteen I would just go and win it. Like I said, I could have fought fifteen more rounds." Notice Ken Norton said that he *thought* that he did enough to earn a draw. There is a difference between one's thoughts, and one's beliefs. The mistake that Ken Norton made was that he went against his beliefs, then put his confidence and his thoughts in the trainer, which cost him the fight. It was later that he published a book titled" *Going the Distance".* The last round of a fight played a major role in going the distance. After Ken Norton was questioned about his loss in the second fight, it was his belief that Ali won the fight because of the final round—however, in his final fight with Ali, he believed that he lost the fight in the last round by listening to his trainer, rather than believing in himself. This gave him a reason to write the book about "Going the distance." A trainer of mine once told me that I should always give all I had on the heavy bag in the final round. I believed that this method should be used in a fight when going the distance. It is about leaving the ring knowing that you gave all you had on the inside. Ken Norton believed that he did not give his best in the last round of his last fight with Muhammad Ali. His belief was that his trainer did not allow him to do so. This is why a Champion should always believe in him or herself, rather than putting all his confidence in the trainer. The trainer only can see what is on the outside, but cannot see the Champion that lives on the inside. In the 1992 Central American and Caribbean Games in Ponce Puerto Rico, while fighting for a medal, I had been in control of the fight. I had my opponent bleeding, knocking him down, and forcing the referee to give him an eight count in the second round. I was ready to finish my opponent, when suddenly the bell rang. In my mind I was ready to go out in the third round to finish my opponent off. As I was in the corner, my boxing coach began telling me, "You are winning the fight, all you need to do is keep jabbing and moving—don't stay close and get caught." I went out in the third round and did exactly what my coach told me, and started jabbing and moving, because I was feeling confident after my coach told me that I was winning. I knew in my mind that I beat my opponent so badly, that even someone who did not see the fight would know that he got a whipping after looking at him. Surprisingly, after the final round of the fight, after hearing the sound of the bell, I looked up in the air on the scorecard; and I was in astonishment. I just could not, and would not believe that the scorecard had me losing the fight by one point. This was when I begin asking questions like, "What happened? What kind of fight are the judges watching?" Even the boxing doctor became curious. That night I was in tears, knowing that I would not receive a medal. I then became very upset at my coach, blaming him for telling me not to get close to my opponent, which made the judges believe that I was a coward, while my opponent was the aggressor in the last round. I then promised myself that I would not listen to my coach's instruction for my next boxing match. Two months later I was in another competition as the Negril Boxing Team had to compete with Cincinnati Ohio Boxing Team. I trained very hard for that fight; in my mind, I did not need a coach, and did not need a corner man, because I was ready to show my coach the Champion that was on the inside. On that fight night, my opponent did not have a chance—it was like a massacre. He went down twice in the second found, and had nothing left for the third round as the bell rang. At the sound of the bell for the third round, he was on his feet, just to fall outside the ring, after I went out with a barrage of punches. To bring the Champion out of you, you have to be ready to go above and beyond; in addition, you have to believe in yourself. Even if you do not have the right trainer, it does not disqualify you from being Champion. There are athletes that had good trainers, yet they are not Champions, while there are athletes who do not have good trainers, yet they are Champions. This then speaks about the athlete's dedication, strength, and belief in his or herself. A true Champion is one that stands alone: even when the battle and the odds are against you. It is not about who you know on the outside—it is about the person that you know living on the inside.

WHEN THE BATTLE IS NOT IN YOUR FAVOR:

To have the word "Champion" as a title, you have to know the game. To bear the name, you have to play the game. In the life of a Champion, there will be times when the battle will be against you—times when the fight may not be in your favor. It could be that you are in a do-or-die situation, and need a knock-out to win. This is when you must prove yourself; and give the audience their money's worth. As a young boy living in Jamaica, I grew up loving to play the sport called Cricket. Cricket is a big sport in Jamaica—it is one of my father's favorites sport. In a one-day match between Jamaica and Barbados (for the Red Stripe Cup Championship), each team had to compete to win in fifty overs—this means that each team would pitch three hundred balls, since each over has six balls to pitch. It happened that Barbados went in as the bats men: the bats man are known to be the person with the bat that tries to hit the ball. Barbados went to bat the ball, and made two 222 runs in fifty balls. This means that Jamaica would need 223 runs to win. It happened that Jamaica had 222 runs, with one final ball to pitch. The person with the bat is known as the "bats man" one that tries to hit the ball, or the batter only option was to hit the ball across the boundary for four runs, or straight over for six runs. This means that the odds were against the bats man, or the batter who was facing the pitcher. The pitch could not bowled the ball too wide, or else it would be ruled a no-ball, which would give the bats man an extra run. The field was well covered to prevent the bats man from hitting the ball across the boundary. The outcome of the game was in the hands of the bats man, and the pitcher, known as the bowler. It happened when the pitcher from Barbados pitched the ball: the Jamaican bats man hit the ball across the boundary for four runs. Jamaica then went on to win the "Red Stripe Cup Champion" 226-225. Both bats man and pitcher would have to prove themselves, because their country was relying on them. In the life of a Champion, sometimes his or her back will seem to be against the rope, and the question becomes: "What do you do when you don't know what to do?" Oftentimes people find themselves in trouble, and in some kind of life's crisis without having the answers. Some seek counsel, while some pray to the Lord for answers. In the life of a Champion, he or she has to be the best in the game, even when the game is not in their favor. A true Champion never loses confidence in his or herself. Some people panic when they are faced with difficulty while driving, then makes matters worse. Even in a losing battle, there is still a chance to win. This means that you have to keep your confidence to overcome the odds and the fear that will be coming against you. Your next weapon for this encounter is your faith A Champion of faith is one that is unmovable and unstoppable. He or she does not believe in the fear, the jeers, or the odds. He rather believes that they are the master of the game, and can turn the situation around, even when it looks impossible—because a Champion believes that all things are possible. If winning is your belief, then you are eventually a winner. This also means that a Champion refuses to lose, because He is in to win. These characteristics are the confidence of a Champion. Although it may look like the battle is not in the Champion's favor, that's not his belief; his or her belief is in themselves as a winner. Whenever the battle is not in the favor of a Champion, it gives him or her the option to prove themselves by digging deep. This is when they will use all the tools, all the techniques, and all the tricks in the book that teaches how to become a winner. Whenever a Champion gives his or her best, it leaves a memory, and also a legacy. Despite the outcome in the battle, the saying will be, "Well done."

One of the many great fights that took place in the sport of boxing was the fight between Champion Floyd "Money" Mayweather and "Sugar"

Shane Mosley. It happened in the second round when the Champion Floyd Mayweather was hit with a big right hand from Shane Mosley. It was a punch that wobbled Mayweather's knee, which could have put him to the canvas. Mayweather took the punch like a true Champion. Some boxing fans thought that Floyd would not be able to recover from such a punch—however, a Champion always has a different thought, and a different outcome in his mind. Floyd Mayweather rallied; he did not panic; but rather kept his composure and his confidence as a Champion. A Champion of confidence knows how to keep his composure. He brings the Champion out, displays his skills, his brilliance, and the gift in him, to bring out the Champion he is on the inside. It was after he rallied back that boxing analyst Larry Merchant commented ,"If Mayweather was not the gifted athlete he is, he would have surely gone down." It did seem as if the fight was not in the Champion's favor. After the punch, however, he showed the heart of a Champion when he came back to win the fight on a unanimous decision. Although the battle may not seem to be in your favor, if you have faith and confidence in yourself, you can turn the battle around by bringing out the Champion in you. Remember, every real fight that you get in; you will have to dig deep to get out. There is a lesson that is going to come out of you. There will be a legacy and some kind of character to teach, and something to tell someone: you have been in a real fight. You might came out with a swollen eye, or a bloody nose, but your swollen eye or your bloody nose will not deny the Champion in you: they will only define your character. Although the battle was not in your favor, and the odds were against you, you came out with the Champion still living in you.

Destined to win:

A winner is one who has the desire to win, even when it looks difficult. Having a desire to win is to see winning as your only outcome.
It is like sleeping, dreaming, and at the same time, winning. You
should be *thinking* winning, and *playing* winning; this then means that
you are *living* winning. Winning must be in your mind. Understand
the importance of winning after you first taste the feeling of losing.
A winner who tastes defeat for the first time will twice make up
for his or her loss. Thinking back to my younger days of boxing, I
remember that I did win my first ten fights. All that was in my mind
was about winning; I thought that it was impossible to be beaten.
My trainer, Robert Harris, said, "I am sorry for anyone who is not
in shape that enters the ring with Paul—your bottom will be on
the grass, because Paul will run over you like a tractor." However,
the day when I lost my first fight was something very hard for me
to accept; it was like swallowing pills without water. Of course I
thought that I won, because winning was always in my mind, I lost
to someone who was known to be the hometown hero, and lost
while in his hometown. I knew that I did train hard for that fight,
but the real training of my life started after losing my first fight. I
often said that you will never know how useful something is, or how
grateful you should be for something that is in your possession until
it is taken away from you. It is like the parable about the lost coin,

written in St. Luke 15:8, or the parable of the prodigal son, verse 11. The woman that lost the coin went the extra mile of lighting a candle and sweeping the house, and when she found the lost coin, she called her neighbors and began to rejoice (St. Luke 15: 8-9). In addition, after the prodigal son lost all his resources and came to the broken point of his life, he was willing to become a slave, just to go back home to his father (verse 18-19.) They have found out the importance of having after losing. You must see your loss as your process to maturity. Never see your loss as your setback—use it as your learning guide to your comeback. It could be that God uses losses, knockdowns, and setbacks to challenge you, to test you, and to bring out the Champion that lives in you. Don't get comfortable with your loss and become a sleeping Champion—use it to awaken the Champion in you. Although I did lose my eleventh fight, it did not stop me from believing in the winner that I am, even to this day. I believe that there is still a winner, and a Champion that lives in me. There are some athletes who, as soon as they lose for the first time, develop fear, which then develops a losing streak. This happens when the mindset is changed. However, you should not let one loss change you from being the winner that God created you to be. You need to have a mindset that tells you, "I am destined to win." This then will force you to push yourself harder. A person with a mindset to win is one that is always aiming to achieve, always ready to receive, one that always coming with something up the sleeves, with a mind that believes. Believing that you are destined to win automatically makes you a Champion in the mind. You could be in the game, but if your mind is not there, you might as well go to where your mind is going. This means, if winning is your destiny, then you will have to set your mind to win. Athletes who became winners are those that have a mind of destiny, a mind that is willing to go above and beyond any circumstances. Remember that the mind sees the ordinary. To have the mind of a Champion, and the mind of a winner, you have to go beyond the natural mind; you must see beyond the ordinary. The mind of a winner is a mind that sees the extra-ordinary. A person who is destined to win is a person whose mind continues to dream. Start dreaming, start believing, and start aiming to become the Champion that God created you to be. Start facing the fear of your life by bringing out the Champion in you. I remember watching a young man as he was in training for the first year playing football; he did not really know the game, but he loved the game, and his desire was all about playing football. Because of his lack of knowledge in knowing the game, it seemed as if the coach was ready to give up on him,—but he refused to let the coach do so, because he did believe in himself. I watched as he was put out of the game and had to watch from the sideline. As I looked at his mother, I could see disappointment in her eyes, as if she was also ready to give up on her son. At one point she told me that she would remove her son from playing football, because she believed that he would do better at soccer. I then let her know that she should not decide for her son, as it was about what her son loved, and what he knew on the inside of him that he was willing to bring out. In addition, I told her to give him time to improve, because he had just started. After one of his practice sessions it seemed as if he did not play, as he left the game looking dry and sad. I remembered that day looking at his mother; she was looking very sad, and was ready to get upset at her son. I then let her know that her son is just going through the process of improvement before his development. At some point it was her son who seemed to build courage, and started to encourage and motivate his mother by saying, "Mom, this is just one game—look and see, next time I am going to do better." I tried to encourage him by telling him that he was a Champion, but he would have to overcome the jeers, discouragement, and disappointment. In the next practice match, the young man was playing as if he was the star of the team, as everyone began yelling his name. He was now ready to bring out the Champion that was in him, and to become the crowd favorite. He was like an all-rounder, making the tackles, taking down the players, and also making touchdowns. The coach and fans that were looking discouraged in him were now seemingly very confident, knowing that he would do well. It was a week later when I went to see the young man playing a real football game for the first time. I was on my feet for most of the game after seeing him playing on the field. I remembered at one point watching him as he kicked the ball down the field, then ran down the field and tackled the running back that caught the ball, taking down the running back, as he was running, trying to head for a touchdown. I later learned that this young man was nine years old, and was also playing the position of a linebacker. Later in the game he made an interception and ran down the field with the ball for a touchdown. Although he was a line-backer, he was able to run with the ball down the field, having the audience, his mother, and myself on our feet shouting. . He made it all the way in the in zone for a touchdown. He is now considered as one of the stars on the team. The Champion that lives in you will have the fans shouting. Despite the times when everyone seemed as if they were discouraged in the young man, he still believed in himself, and kept his promise that he would do better—and that was exactly what he did. This was because of the belief that he had in himself, and the love that he had for playing football. A mind that is destined to win is a mind that will improve. He proved that he had a mind that refused to be discourage, and a mind that refused to quit. Whenever your mind refuses to be discouraged, you will use the same mind to encourage the minds of those who try to discourage you. In addition, people will start believing in the Champion in you.

THE RESUME OF A CHAMPION:

People often times view champions, admire Champions, and welcome Champions because of their impressive records. This could totally be wrong, because some so-called Champions fought fights that were fixed, and made their way to the top because of the managers and promoters that tried to protect them. Some win by a lucky punch, hometown decision, or a fixed decision. However, a real Champion is one who defies the odds, one who knows what it means to fight back, and one who is determined to fight, even when the odds are not in his or her favor. Not because you might have lost your first fight—that does not disqualify you from being a Champion. It is when you are ready to prove yourself to the world and are willing to overcome obstacles and the fear that life often brings your way. A Champion with a good resume is one who went through many battles that were not in his or her favor—and not only a physical battle. This is one who has overcome the storms of life, having been through all the things that the world throws at them. They are willing to stand and embrace those things, and become victorious, rather than becoming a victim. Muhammad Ali is thought to be one of the greatest boxers in the sport; however, it was not because of his record that many thought that he was the greatest. It was because he beat all the fighters that beat him in his previous fights. Although he was stripped of his title after refusing to go to war, and had to go through a setback, those things did not prevent him from being a Champion on the inside. To prove yourself, you must be willing to clean up your resume. You should not leave unfinished business; you have to be willing to face your fear with faith. In addition, Muhammad always had confidence in himself. Even in his loss, he had confidence, because it was his learning process for redemption. One way to bring the Champion out of you is to be willing to face your giant of fear. To face your giant of fear, you don't need a perfect score—you must first list in your resume the word of God. If you have the word of God on your side, then you are in it to win it. It is not the many losses that you have on your resume that matter—what really matters is that you were able to get up and get through all of them. The Bible tells us that a righteous man fall seven times, but he rises up again, as written in Proverbs 24:16. Before David went up to face the giant Goliath, he already did have a resume, and although it did not look perfect, he did have some valley experience. His introduction was the word of God that said it all. To back up his resume, he did kill a lion and a bear with his bare hands; furthermore, he let the king know that it was the Lord who delivered the lion and bear into his hands, and the giants would become as one of them. He developed his resume from his valley experience. Don't become a victim because of the things that you have been through—not because someone else's resume looks better than yours, not because you are in the back of the line, or because you are behind on the score card. All you need to do is stay in the race, and stay in the fight. It is not about the energy, or what your opponent displays on the outside—it is about what is reserved on the inside. Remember, "The race is not for the swift, or the battle for the strong, but for the one that endures to the end." Fighters that enter the ring sometimes enter with names like the Hammer, the Machine gun, or the Destroyer, etc. Some enter with a mask, some with a fancy robe with their names on the back of their robes. Some enter with their face looking mean. The referee then calls both fighters to have a stare-down; each fighter looks at the other for a sign of fear. There are many fighters that lose the fight in their own mind because of fear. Some lose because of the other fighter's resume. However, you should not let the resume put fear in you, not because of your opponent's trainer, or the fighters that he fought and won—it is what you know on the inside of you. You must first believe in yourself, and the Champion that lives in you. When I was a fighter in Boston Massachusetts, a former trainer became upset because I went with another trainer. His plan was to teach me a lesson by starting to train another fighter. His plan was to train his fighter to fight me. A former sparring partner of mine told the trainer that the fighter that he was training would not be able to beat me, because he sparred with both of us before, and knew what the outcome will be. The trainer then asked him, "Who do you think is the trainer?" He thought that he was the one who made me the Champion that I was, but I was already a Champion before I met him. That night in the fight, I won a unanimous decision on all the judges' scorecards. My sparring partner went back and said to the trainer, "I told you that your fighter would not win!" He then said to my sparring partner, "Yea, he is a tough kid." My sparring partner was the one who told me these things after the fight. I say this because, if you are a Champion, it is not because of your trainer—your trainer helps you to correct your mistakes, but the Champion is already on the inside of you. When fighting in the boxing ring, your trainer cannot help you when you are in trouble. He or she cannot feel your pain. Being in that ring is totally different than being on the basketball court. On the court, you have your teammates to help; you might not be able to make the shot, but you can pass the ball to someone that is open. You might have a better shooter than yourself. You win on that court as a team, but in that ring, if you are hurt and in pain, or if you are on the canvas for the second or third time, it will prove the real person in you. This is where your instinct, your determination, and everything on the inside of you must come in play. Your resume from college, or your previous jobs, prove your character. The things that you came through proves the person who you. It is not about the person that people see on the outside, it is about the person on the inside. Before you judge the cover, or the looks, you must first know what's on the inside by reading the book. As a fighter, there were many fighters who turned down fights because of their opponent's record. A fighter can be undefeated, yet he has never been in a real fight. He or she may have what seemed to be a perfect record, yet all their fights were fighting bums. This means they have never been taken to their limits to bring out their best. Some fighters go inside the ring just for a payday, hoping to get an easy punch then take a knee so that they can walk away with some money. A real fighter or Champion does not just fight for a payday. You can never pay a Champion to take a knee—he is one that would rather die trying. In 1990, when I first won the Welter Weight Champion in Jamaica, I was in the first round when I threw a left hook and pulled a muscle in my left arm. From there on, I could not throw a left jab, because my left arm was considered useless. My opponent was approximately six foot two, and I was five foot nine. I had to turn the fight into a slugfest. I remembered some of my teammates, including my trainer, yelling, "Paul, use your jab!" However, I could not talk, because of the mouthpiece. It was after going back to the corner that I told my trainer that my left hand was injured. Although my left hand was hurting, I did refuse to give up. I remembered my trainer once told me, "A winner never quits, and a quitter never wins." Although I fought that night with one hand that did not deny me from bringing out the real person in me, and that was to become a Champion. It again happened in the New England Championship in the year 1995. It happened in Boston Massachusetts at the beginning of the Championship; just after I finished fighting the elimination bout, I was told that I had to fight again the same night. I fought twice in one night—the first fight of the night, and also the fifth fight. I won both, then went on to win three more fights, including the New England Championship, and the award for most outstanding fighter for the tournament. It is not about the way the fight looks on the external, not because of the resume—it is what you have on the inside. You must be ready to dig deep, even when it is not in your favor.

THE LEGACY OF A CHAMPION:

Champions are those who always will be remembered by their characteristics, their skills, or something very outstanding and spectacular. It is one who does not just leave as the ordinary, but one who leaves as the extra-ordinary, the unusual—one who leaves an impression on the mind of the audience. The audience hopes to see the return, or someone who will walk in that legacy. There must be something to remember about a Champion that pleases his or her audience, some kind of impression of his or her characteristics. It could be skills, confidence, brilliance, or even courage. He or she is one that goes out on a high note. A true Champion does not go out intimidated, or overrated, but one that goes out as one of the greatest. A champion that goes out as the greatest is one like Muhammad Ali. Many said that he was the greatest, even to this day. One of the many reasons why I admire Muhammad Ali is his confidence. Anyone that has confidence believes that a Champion is on the inside. One of Muhammad Ali's toughest fights was against George Foreman. Foreman was known to be a strong fighter, one who could knock out any fighter in any given round. Many thought that fighting George Foreman was a big risk for Muhammad Ali, but a fighter that has self-belief never sees themselves as in danger, but always sees a way out. He sees his way out in the mind. A confident fighter is one who fight with his or her mind. This was what I saw in watching the

fight between George Foreman and Muhammad Ali. Ali fought with
his mind, while Foreman fought with his strength. Although Foreman
would try pinning Ali on the rope to hurt him, Ali was talking to
Foreman with words like, "Is that all you can do?" or "You punch
like a chicken." Perhaps Foreman had hurt Ali a few times, but a
Champion that fights with his or her mind never shows any sign to
his opponent—he'd rather let his opponent believe that he is just
having fun in the match. With Ali using his mind, Foreman got more
frustrated, and tried to be more aggressive. However, this was Ali's
plan—to take Foreman out of his game. Ali sometimes stayed in the
rope to pretend as if he were in trouble, but he was only using his
mind so that Foreman would punch himself away. A fighter that uses
his or her mind waits for the right time. It was later in the seventh
round that Foreman became very tired. Ali knew that moment was
coming, and was just waiting for the right time to throw the perfect
shot. It happened in the eighth round when Muhammad Ali caught
George Foreman with what I called the perfect shot, which sent
George Foreman to the canvas, who was later counted out. Foreman
was considered one of the greatest fighters during those days, but
losing to Ali gave Ali the name as the best, which later made boxing
fans believe that he was one of the greatest of all time. Ali went out
with a name, and became one of the greatest in the Hall of Fame. He
leaves a legacy which will always be remembered, and is a fighter
who went back to beat all the opponents that he had lost to in previous fights. A true Champion may go out with injury, may have been
jeered, or have had some kind of setbacks, but he or she will return
with pride. It was on June 20, 1967 when Muhammad Ali was sen-
tenced to five years in prison, because he refused to go in the mili-
tary. Despite the setback that he encountered, it did not deprive him
from becoming the Champion that was on the inside. On October
30, 1974, he returned—after spending five years in prison—to fight
one of the most dangerous and strongest fighters of the era: George
Foreman. He came away with the victory. This proves that a true
Champion never changes, whether going out, or coming in. In addition, he showed up to meet the fans' expectations, and to give them
the Champion that they came out to see. A Champion also leaves the

audience wanting more, because of the display of skill, the pride, and the confidence; they prove to the world that a true Champion never disappears, because a Champion lives on the inside. Despite what he has to deal with on the outside, he or she will come back to prove themselves to all that would deprive the Champion on the inside. Another great Champion that I truly admired as a role model is Sugar Ray Leonard. He went into retirement in 1982. This was because of a detached retina that he suffered during a fight with Thomas "The Hitman" Hearns. This happened sometime on September 16, 1981 at Caesar's Palace; the two fought a gruesome and epic battle to unify the world welterweight championship. They fought before a crowd of 23, 618 and a worldwide TV audience of some 300 million. I viewed that fight as a "brawler versus a boxer" as Sugar Ray Leonard boxed from a distance, while Thomas Hearns became the stalker. At the end of five rounds, Sugar Ray Leonard had a growing swelling under his left eye as Hearns constantly was throwing jabs; he had built a comfortable lead. Despite the swollen eye and the advantage of Thomas Hearns, Sugar Ray Leonard would not throw in the towel, and he would not let the difficulty of the fight stop him from bringing out the Champion that was on the inside; he would bear the name as the Sugar man of boxing that he was. He became more aggressive, hurt Thomas Hearns in the sixth round with a left hook to the chin, and gave Hearns a severe beating in rounds six and seven. However, Thomas Hearns also proved the Champion that was in him when he rallied back, and started jabbing and moving; he was able to pile up some points. Afterward, it was Sugar Ray Leonard who became the stalker, while Hearns had to go on his feet and start dancing away from Sugar Ray Leonard. Hearns managed to win the ninth round up to the twelve on all three judges' scorecards. However, the Champion in my favorite fighter Sugar Ray Leonard was not done. Although his left eye was badly swollen and battered, he was able to explode with a barrage of combinations that sent Hearns crashing through the ropes in the thirteenth round. After staggering Thomas Hearns with an over hand right, Ray Leonard then pinned Hearns against the ropes, and unleashed some vicious and furious punches, which forced the referee Davey Pearl to stop the fight. Sugar Ray Leonard was awarded the unified World Welterweight Championships, although Thomas Hearns was leading on points, by scores 124-122---125-122---125-121. This proved Sugar Ray Leonard as one who defied the pain, the odds, the jeers and critics to pull off a win in one of his most difficult fights of his life. It was after this gruesome fight that Sugar Ray Leonard had to go into retirement, because of his left eye that was badly damaged, which made it difficult for him to see. He went through a setback for four years, which many thought that he would not be able to come back from in order to perform as a Champion. Some thought that his career was over. However, Leonard proved to the world what the legacy of a Champion is by changing many thoughts and beliefs when he returned to the ring to fight one of the most furious, vicious, and dangerous fighters, "Marvelous" Marvin Hagler. On April 6, 1987, the sugar man of boxing, Sugar Ray Leonard, decided to take on "Marvelous Marvin Hagler. I remembered so much about the fight as if it were just a few days back. It was four days after my twenty-first birthday. I'd saved the money to order the fight on Pay per View. On that day, I had exactly sixty Jamaican dollars, which was the cost. Although I did not have any more money than the cost of the fight, I was willing to do whatever it takes to see these two great Champions because of my favorite fighter and Champion. I still remember the skills that were displayed by the Sugar man of boxing. Many people did believe that Sugar Ray Leonard would not stand a chance against Marvin Hagler. However, I always observed that he was a fighter that used his brain, one that was very smart—one with confidence, who believed in himself. After four years of retirement and setback, after he suffered an eye retina, he was still willing to make a comeback, and take on one of the toughest fighters of all time. This tells me that a real Champion is proven by the heart, and the confidence that he or she shows in themselves. As I reflect on the fight, I can remember seeing Sugar Ray as he shuffled, and stays on his toes, dancing on his feet, grinning and showing his teeth, while the fans celebrated the beat of the heat. Although "Marvelous" Marvin Hagler was known as the one that wore the crown, the ruler of the town, pound for pound, the master of round by round, trying to knock Ray Leonard to the ground, Ray would not go down. He came out of retirement, prepared himself, went through some training, and made his way back to the ring to prove the Champion that was in him. He knew the game, claimed the name, and made it to the Hall of Fame. A Champion who believes in him or herself will prove to the world that nothing is impossible to those that believe in themselves. They will be the ones that enter the stage with loud applause, and leave the audience excited, wanting more. A true Champion is one that is proven after overcoming what many people say will be difficult, going above and beyond one's belief, and proving that there is nothing that is impossible, if there is a Champion in you. Saul, who was the first king of Israel, did not believe that a small-looking shepherd boy by the name of David would have a chance against a nine-foot, nine-inch-tall giant whose name was Goliath. To defeat your giant of fear to bring the king or the Champion out of you, you must be willing to go above and beyond the ordinary, in order to bring the Champion out. In other words, you have to be able to maximize your limitation. You will let people know that it is not the way you look on the outside, and that there is an unknown, an unseen aspect on the inside that is ready to be awakened. If you study the life of Sugar Ray Leonard, you will notice that he was not one that looked like a fighting monster or a beast ; still, he was no pushover in the ring—he was known to be a very good finisher, and was very quick on his feet, with flashy head movements, lighting speed, and was known to be very intelligent. He was not someone that looked muscular or tall. When he fought against "Marvelous Marvin Hagler, and Thomas "Hitman" Hearns, he was five foot eight, while Thomas Hearns was six foot two. Sugar Ray Leonard was not one that seemed to match the strength of Marvin Hagler; he did not have that tough look on the outside. He looked to be ta normal athlete—this was the reason why many people did not see him qualified and capable of surviving against Marvin Hagler. But Sugar Ray's strength was on the inside. He proved them wrong. You cannot judge someone by their appearance —you define a Champion by what he or she has on the inside, which I will discuss more in the next chapter. The legacy of a Champion is one that goes out high, one who goes out with pride, and one who goes out with his or her hands raised high. They are those that raise the applause, meet the cost, and prove that true Champions do not lose. They prove to the fans, and to the odds, that a true Champion is one that lives in the heart.

THE HOPE AND LEGACY OF A CHAMPION:

The hope and legacy of a Champion gives the audience the hope and the confidence that nothing is impossible if your mind is made up to endure pain and hardship in whatever you pursue. It takes pain, faith, and anguish, along with dedication, resilience, and perseverance. You can look at the fulfillment, the legacy, and hope that was distinguished by the late Nelson Mandela. He had shown the meaning of hope as a true Champion, and a freedom fighter, and what it means to go through struggles in fighting for freedom. Although he had to spend twenty-seven years of his life in prison, it did not stop him from believing in himself as a true hero, and a freedom fighter. He proved to his audience the meaning of hope, and leaves a legacy: you have to believe in yourself—it is worth the cost. The hope that he showed through his imprisonment for twenty-seven years, and the legacy that he left will be remembered. Despite what he had to go through in prison, nothing could deprive him of what he believed. He defied the odds, kept his faith, kept his hope alive, and endured persecution and affliction to define the Champion that he was. He left prison and rose to the occasion and the achievement of becoming president of South Africa. Truly he had proven that it does not matter what the odds are, or the things that you have to overcome in life. It does not matter your setbacks, or your downfalls: because those things cannot defy you of your destiny—they define your characteristics, and the Champion that lives in you. His remarkable comeback from prison to president leaves hope, and a legacy to his peers, his followers, and a nation that whatever you desires are, and whatever you decide to become, will decide your destiny. Those years in prison were just his defining moments of his life by going through the process that qualified him for the position that God ordained for his life. The trials, the setbacks, and the many challenges that you go through in your daily life, those are things that God uses to try you, to equip you, and to get you ready for the assignment that He has for you to fulfill. After Nelson Mandela fulfilled his assignment, his assessment test in his prison, he could fulfill the task and the role of a president and a freedom fighter. It was because of the freedom that he was willing to fight for: that forced him to go to prison. The Bible tells us, "The greatest love that one can give is to lay down your life for a friend," as written in St. John 15:13. This was the example that Jesus gave—He laid down His life, so that mankind would have life. Nelson Mandela was willing to go to prison to bear the cost of fighting for freedom. He leaves hope, and a legacy to encourage everyone, and to show the meaning of faith. "You can do the impossible if you believe in your faith." His life was a living testimony that narrates to the life of Joseph in the Bible. Joseph suffered a setback and went to prison, as written Genesis 39:20-23—however it was through those defining moments of Joseph's life that the Lord prepared him in the prison. He was later removed from prison to become the prince of Egypt, as written in Genesis 41:41-44. It was through Joseph's imprisonment that God used him as the one to bring hope to his family, and to provide food for them in the time of famine. To define hope, and then leave a legacy, you indeed must go through a time of bewilderment, or some defining moment that will define your character, and the Champion that you are on the inside. The things that you must go through in life will either break you or make you. You have to believe in yourself that you are not going to break down, but rather break through. It was the hope, the belief and the faith that Joseph had in God that brought him through the things that he had to go through that defined him as a leader and a hero in the Bible. It was through Nelson Mandela's faith, his beliefs, and the courage that he displayed that gave him the ability to leave a legacy, and the hope to those who admire him. Before you can claim faith, you have to first live the life, because without works, faith is dead. Although Nelson Mandela died, his faith still lives today. In his life's journey, he was not distracted in his endeavor, because of a setback. He did not let his prison deny him of his freedom: because he proved the hope that lived on the inside. He took his aim and position for his purpose. He used his setback in prison as a learning experience to prove to the world that every setback is just a set-up for preparation for making a comeback, with an impact. He did not leave prison as a victim—he left prison as the victor, and a conqueror—one who rises from a dead situation to teach what it means to fight for freedom. His life was an example of the life of David: one who was willing to stand in the gap, and face a giant that comes to deprive Israel of their freedom in serving God. In addition, his life leaves a portrayed the life of Jesus Christ: who was willing to lay down His life, so that life could be given. The hope and legacy that he left really creates an impact in life, which also makes a difference in people's lives today.

DON'T WATCH THE LOOK:
READ THE BOOK:

Many people view life on the outside world, believing in the natural, and the things that they see. However, this could totally be misguided and misleading. This was the reason why Eve was beguiled by the Devil in the garden of Eden, because the Devil told her about the fruit, and that if she ate it, she would become wise like gods, knowing good from evil (Genesis 3:5). Of course God did already warned Adam about the danger of touching the tree, or eating the fruit of the tree that was in the midst of the Garden of Eden (verse 2-3). However, because of the temptation and the look of the fruit, Eve followed the Devil's advice, then get herself in trouble. This is to let you know that looks can be very deceiving.. There are fighters that I knew that chose opponents who seemed as if they had messed-up boxing records, but then they found themselves in trouble after the bell rang. You cannot estimate a fighter because of the record, you have to first know the opponents that he or she lost to. Some fighters that seem to have a boxing record that does not look perfect may have lost all their fights to Champions, which means that they are not push-overs, but are always aiming for the top. I can remember some years back, a former boxing teammate of mine was in the Contender. The prize for winning the final was five hundred thousand dollars.

On the way to the final four, he was given the chance to choose the fighter that he wished to fight. He then went and chose the fighter that had the worst record, including eight losses. It happened that the same fighter with eight losses went on to win the Contender, and five hundred thousand dollars. The reason why he chose that opponent was because of his record. Because some people watch the look, then go after the things that look good, some are left hurt, broken, and in tears. Just like Eve, they then found out that it was the wrong decision. A certain co-worker with whom I once worked at a hotel as a waiter came back to apologize after misjudging me. It happened as we were working as waiters—this person did not allow me to come and help in his station, although he got very busy a few times. I did not know the reason why he would not allow me, even when I had no guest in my station. I later found out that he thought I would take up the tips that the guest would leave him at the table. It happened after we became friends that we would work together as a team. This was when he said to me, "I thought that you would steal my money, because you are from Jamaica, and that's what I've heard that Jamaicans like to do." He then apologized to me, because he had been watching me, but then found out that I was honest, and not the person that he thought as people say, in regards to Jamaicans. Before you judge someone, or say something mean, you must first test the person, because whatever is in you will come out if you have been tested, or have been pushed to your limit. This is why a Champion must be pushed. "Push until something happens." Whatever comes out of you when there is nothing left in you will demonstrate the real you that is left inside. This is why you should always be who you really are, and the person that God created you to be. You sometimes don't know the person that is watching you—you never know where life will sometimes take you. Be ready at all times to go the extra mile; be ready to face the unexpected, because you cannot judge the book by its cover. This is the same with a Champion. You don't know what he has to offer, and you may not know his or her best punch, strength or weakness. You could be in for just a round or two, which means you are in for a surprise. This means that you must always be aware, be prepared, and come expecting to go twelve rounds, fifteen rounds, or even a marathon. A Champion does not show up with half a tank—their tank will always be full, and ready to overflow. This is why you cannot watch the look without knowing what's on the inside. Although it may seem as if a Champion doesn't have the tools, the requirements, or the resources from the external view, don't under-estimate him or her, as there is something behind the scene. This is why you cannot watch the look—read the book. Whenever you are in a fight with a Champion, you are in the fight of your life; in addition, you will be in for a surprise. The reason he or she does not prove who they are on the outside is because the real Champion lives on the inside. The outside may look like a humble lamb, or even a little chicken, but on the inside there could be a roaring lion, a sleeping lion, just waiting to be awakened. Most people that go down are usually the ones that makes the most noise—those are the ones who like to show their muscles. This was the example shown between David and Goliath. It was Goliath who came posing himself for forty days (1 Samuel 17:16). He was the one who came out asking for a fight; he was the one who showed up daily with muscles and the instruments for battle. He was the one that judged David's countenance, as written in verse 42. He was the one who called out David when he said, "Come to me, and I will give thy flesh unto the fowls of the air, and to the beasts of the field." (1 Samuel 17:44 KJV). Although Goliath came to put up a fight, judged David by his looks, and called him out, it was David who had the shot with the final word, in verses 45-49. Goliath did show up by his looks, expressed himself, judged David by his looks, and cursed David by his God,. He did not know the God that lived in David. He did not know that a king and a Champion was living on the inside of David. This is the reason why you cannot watch the look, and must read the book. Don't look at the giant from the outside—he comes to intimidate you by his looks. However, his inside is duplicate, weak, and is ready to go down—not because of the size or the height of the mountain, because if you have faith on the inside, you can climb over it. Your mountain cannot move over you, but you can climb over your mountain. All you need to do is let the faith in you work for you in bringing the Champion out.

ACKNOWLEDGEMENTS:

To my children, Joshua and Jessica Hillman, It is my earnest honor and pleasure to acknowledge both of you. I want to thank you both for believing in me. You two push me to bring out the Champion within, and to write about the Champion in you. Of course I observe a Champion in both of you. I remember times gone when I was feeling weak, and had to go down on my knees. You were both there praying with me, asking God to give Dad the victory. I remember the times when I was doing my physical training, with you Jessie in my arm, with the other one pulling your brother Josh up the hill in the wagon, as I was building strength and endurance. Truly, you two play a part during those days in my training schedule. When I was feeling weak, you both helped me to feel strong, and when I was feeling down, you also helped me to stand strong like a real Champion. You both give me privilege, knowledge and courage to believe that there is a Champion in me. I am so proud of you two, Josh and Jessy, and love you two from the very bottom of my heart—a love that will never depart, the agape and unconditional love, as the love of God. So proud to be your Dad, and to have you two as my son and daughter. To Keya, and her mother Elmon Ray: Thank you for all that you have done for me. Keya, without you: I would not be the person that I am today. You were the one who told me that I had to go back to school. There were many times in life when I get discouraged; you always encourage me. I never forget the day you told me, "You are smarter than you think." You have blessed me in so many ways. I owe you a lot. I thank God for the beautiful children of ours. I am so grateful and excited, especially seeing our son Joshua preaching his first sermon at the age of fifteen years old. Of course I know that he leapt from off our backs. I know that someday our daughter Jessica will be preaching too. You and Grandma have done so many good things in life. You have helped me to be the man that I am, and the father that I am. In addition, you both have also helped me to be the Champion that I am. I love you both from the very depths of my heart. Keya, you are one of the best mothers that I know in raising our children. I am truly blessed to be their father, and thank God for you. It is because of you, my children, the love, the care, and the mother you are that push me to work so hard. Continue to be the person you are. I love you, Grandma, and the kids, and I know that God loves you best.

Paul R. Hillman.

To my Pastor, Clifford C.S Clarke,

Greetings to you, man of God. You have paved the way, and have made the path straight. You have opened up a fountain that leads to the floodgate. For those that are willing to come, after having been broken, you gave them an invitation, and the doors are always open. God has sent you to those that are afflicted, those that are wounded, and those that are isolated, and seem to be in captivity. You came to give them a message, and to set them free. You leave them with a word that says, "Let the redeemed of the Lord say so, whom He hath redeemed from the hands of the enemy." (Psalm 107:2) Continue to lead, to teach, and to preach in season, and out of season. I pray that God will continue to strengthen you, and to keep you flourishing in season and out of season.

Paul R. Hillman,
Associate Pastor.

For those who desire to become Champion, you can if you believe in yourself. The only way to become a Champion is to be like a Champion, do whatever you see a Champion do, and never forget—whatever you do in life, always put God first in your life; if God is in your life, then you are a Champion. Remember that the scripture tells us, "I can do all things through Christ which strengthened me." (Philippians 4:13) This means that there is power within you; it is you who is the one to bring the power on the outside, and prove yourself to be the Champion that God created you to be. Start to dig deep, search yourself, and ask yourself, "What is my gift? What are some of the things that I find myself doing best?" After you ask yourself, you then search yourself and put yourself to the test. The Champion in you may seem to be your biggest challenge, because the only person that can beat you, is you. This means, you can be your biggest source of fear. If you have never pushed yourself out of yourself, then you will never know the strength in you, or the distance that you can go. The real you is not you when you are thinking of yourself, and who you are. The real you is *you*, when you are not aware that you are doing more than you expect. It is like walking a long distance without thinking of the journey: after thinking about it, you then surprise yourself about the distance that you reach. You can only be who God created you to be when you are willing to let go of yourself, without thinking of who you are. Thinking of yourself or your journey will shorten your imagination of going above and beyond. Always be ready to go higher, always be willing to go further, even to the limits of touching the sky—it all begins by believing in yourself.

CPSIA information can be obtained at www.ICGtesting.com
Printed in the USA
LVOW08s0901050516

486450LV00001BA/27/P